Other Voices
Other Lives

Praise for
Other Voices, Other Lives

The poet Grace Cavalieri is also a truly generous friend of poetry and poets. In her writing and all she does her large-minded generosity shines. It's a blessing to American poetry that this radiant, giving spirit, with her appropriate first name, is there in our capital city: a light amid fog.

—*Robert Pinsky*

Most generous, ever-enthusiastic Grace Cavalieri, who has honored so many other poets through decades of thoughtful inquiry and deep listening, is herself the most astonishing voice. We listen with profound gratitude to her magnificence.

—*Naomi Shihab Nye*

Poetry, drama, the interview—Grace Cavalieri has mastered all of these forms with intelligence, imagination, and a gift for language. Her wide-ranging work is beautifully crafted and always alive with emotional resonance.

"Each of us has a pond. Mine is deep," she writes in one of her poems, and she could be speaking of this impressive and necessary collection.

—*Linda Pastan*

Grace Cavalieri has quietly written an amazing body of work that is a testament to her own unique vision and understanding of the world around us. Open *Other Voices, Other Lives* and you will feel the warmth of the sun, you will encounter the breath of oceans wafting over you and in the darkest of times, you will encounter starlight. Read this volume; recommend this volume, then re-read this volume. With each encounter, you will be silently rewarded. Of this I am sure.

—*Herbert Woodward Martin*

Gleaned from a life of service and attentive love for language, this collection of Grace Cavalieri's work enables us to dance a slow dance with an artist and curator who again and again touches our minds and our hearts with her words and generosity of spirit.

Cavalieri's poems and plays are woven through with amazement, wonder, tenderness, and grief. They are works of liberation and love, independence and community. She writes in many voices because she understands the deep value of our multiple-voiced humanity and the bridges that such voices create to help us cross to greater understanding, greater compassion, and greater love.

—*Michael S. Glaser*

Also by Grace Cavalieri

With (Somondoco Press, 2016)

Life Upon the Wicked Stage (New Academia/Scarith, 2015)

The Mandate of Heaven (Bordighera Press, 2014)

The Man Who Got Away (New Academia/Scarith, 2014)

Cosa farei per amore: Poesie dalla voce di Mary Wollstonecraft (Forest Woods Media, 2013)

Gotta Go Now (Casa Menendez Press, 2012)

Millie's Sunshine Tiki Villas: A Novella in Verse (Casa Menendez Press, 2011)

Sounds Like Something I Would Say (Casa Menendez Press, 2010)

Navy Wife (Casa Menendez Press, 2010)

Anna Nicole: Poems (Casa Menendez Press, 2008)

Water on the Sun: Acqua sul sole (Bordighera Press, 2006), translated by Maria Enrico

What I Would Do for Love (Jacaranda Press, 2004)

Greatest Hits, 1975–2000 (Pudding House Press, 2002)

Cuffed Frays and Other Works (Argonne House Press, 2001)

Sit Down, Says Love (Argonne House Press, 1999)

Heart on a Leash (Red Dragon Press, 1998)

Pinecrest Rest Haven (The Word Works, 1998)

Migrations: Poems (Vision Library, 1995)

Trenton (Belle Mead Press, 1990)

Bliss (Hillmunn Roberts Publishing, 1986)

Swan Research (The Word Works, 1979)

Body Fluids (Bunny and Crocodile Press, 1976)

Why I Cannot Take a Lover (Washington Writers Publishing House, 1975)

EDITED VOLUMES

Lark: 50 Poems by Kim Sang Hoon (Shoulder Friends Press, 2016)

Korean Sky: A Memoir, by Dai Sil Kim Gibson (Shoulder Friends Press, 2015)

Iowa Sky: A Memoir, by Donald D. Gibson (Shoulder Friends Press, 2013), compiled and annotated by Dai Sil Kim Gibson

British GI Brides in America: Among the Alien Corn, by Joyce Varney (Forest Woods Media, 2013)

Do Unto Others, by Robert Varney (Forest Woods Media, 2012)

Looking for Don by Dai Sil Kim Gibson (Forest Woods Media, 2012)

The Poet's Cookbook: Recipes from Germany, Poems by 33 American Poets with German Translations (Goethe-Institut and Forest Woods Media, 2010), co-edited with Sabine Pascarelli

The Poet's Cookbook: Recipes from Tuscany, Poems by 28 Italian and American Poets (Bordighera Press, 2009), co-edited with Sabine Pascarelli

Cycles of the Moon Vine, by Jean Emerson (Forest Woods Media Productions, 1997)

WPFW 89.3 FM Poetry Anthology: The Poet and the Poem (Bunny and the Crocodile Press, 1992)

Dedicated to Ken Flynn, always and beyond; and to our children: Cindy, Colleen, Shelley, and Angel; our grandchildren, Rachel, Elizabeth, Sean, and Joe; and now our great-grandchild Dylan.

Grateful love to Rose Solari and James J. Patterson for their friendship, personal elegance, and professional integrity.

Contents

Language and Love:
The Work of Grace Cavalieri

*B*efore I met Grace Cavalieri, I had already fallen in love with her voice. I was in my early twenties when I began tuning into her weekly radio show, *The Poet and the Poem*, broadcast then on Washington D.C.'s blues and jazz station, WPFW. Grace is a nimble interviewer—erudite and playful, sassy and wise—but what struck me most about her was the passion I heard in every word she uttered. This was clearly a woman for whom poetry was an urgent necessity, a sacred art. I was just beginning to take my own poetry seriously, to believe, despite family pressure, that I too might establish a life for myself devoted to its practice. *Do it*, she seemed to be saying to me. *What could be more beautiful or more important?*

I began to look for her at literary readings and events around the city. She wasn't hard to spot. Wherever Grace is, there is always a lively crowd around her. When she reads from her own work, she manifests that same brilliant combination that had won me over on the radio: she can be puckish and witty when setting up a poem, but when she reads it, she speaks simply, from deep inside the poem itself. She doesn't take herself too seriously, but she gives poetry the weight it deserves.

One afternoon, shortly before my first book was published, I spotted Grace in the audience at one of my own readings. Her presence made me stand up a little straighter; I wanted, even more than usual, to do my best. Grace made a point of speaking to me afterward, commenting with great specificity and insight on the work I'd presented. Her praise made me glow. She said she'd be keeping an eye on me.

Soon, she was sending me encouraging postcards, suggesting I send work to this magazine or that grant program. These were written in what I soon came to recognize as Grace's signature style, with colorful inks and peppered with stickers of hearts, butterflies, and birds. And I was far from the only one receiving such treasures. When meeting other writers, I've found that Grace's name functions like a calling card. Poets from Seattle to San Francisco, from Miami to Manhattan not only admire her work but have stories to tell about her generosity, her enthusiasm, her wise critique of poems that haven't quite found their final form. Her gift for friendship and for building community is legendary, yet her attentions always feel very personal.

What is most astonishing to me is how she finds time for so much outreach and nurturing in the midst of a busy career she's built by hand. While many other poets of her stature have found perches at universities or foundations, Grace has carved out an independent path, guest teaching here and there, forging connections between diverse literary groups, launching off-Broadway plays. She's a tireless reviewer of poetry, prose, and drama. And of course, there's the radio show, which she prepares for meticulously every week. A constant refrain from those who have been interviewed by Grace—me included—is how deeply and thoroughly she has read their work. Her interview subjects range from poet laureates to as-yet-unknown writers, and she gives each the same warm, rapt attention.

The range and variety of Grace's career is mirrored in the work itself. Like Anne Sexton and Carolyn Kizer, she is a fearless explorer of female experience. Whether writing in personae—as the twentieth-century pop star Anna Nicole Smith, say, or the eighteenth-century feminist Mary Wollstonecraft—or from her own life, Grace's work plumbs, with precision and not a little anger, what it means to live in a world still mostly shaped and ruled by men. Many writers might build a career on this alone.

But Grace moves swiftly among themes, forms, and schools. Take for example her suite of experimental poems, "Cora," in which she riffs off of William Carlos Williams's *Kora in Hell: Improvisations*, a dreamlike, book-length sequence first published in 1920. Grace navigates Williams's avant-garde territory with a playfulness not present in the original. Another sequence, "Millie's Sunshine Tiki Villas," veers from surrealism to slapstick in its depiction of a Florida retirement village.

Grace's work also gently and movingly navigates that subject considered to be a specialty of poets: loss. John Keats, the great celebrant of nature's promise and its passing, would surely find a kindred spirit in the author of the poem "Carciofi," who writes,

> One by one things fall away,
> everything but the sweet earth itself.
> Already this year he has watched the nest's
> careful brush of twigs lose a summer song.

This elegiac tone comes through perhaps most beautifully in Grace's poems for her late husband, the Navy pilot, artist, and inventor Ken Flynn. The poem "Everything Is Smaller Than the Truth" begins "Knowing the worst, he is gone,/I still try to learn the way of sleep," and traces the writer's grieving through a restless night to the breaking dawn. The poem concludes with lines that will ring true for anyone who has lost a loved one:

> …What language is this
> with its different group of birds
>
> telling me the day, its terrible truth,
> is going on before me.

IN A BODY OF WORK so varied, what are the thematic throughlines? As I read and reread the work contained here, I found three that I believe are crucial to Grace's worldview.

One is the importance of work. Grace's poems and plays are filled with people who derive their sense of meaning from their work in the world, from the author's grandfather picking artichokes in Tuscany to Mary Wollstonecraft's fierce determination to be taken seriously as a writer. In the poem "Work Is My Secret Lover," Grace takes on the conflict between domestic obligations and the pull of art, writing of playing the role of good hostess during the Christmas holidays, while

"Work waited patiently/among ornaments gleaming like a groom."

Another consistent theme-with-variations is love. But make no mistake: though Grace's love poems brim with tenderness, they are never sentimental. Love, in her work, is both magic and effort, Cupid's fleet arrow and Penelope's patient weaving. Take for example Mr. and Mrs. P, the central characters of the Pinecrest Rest Haven poems and play. Because of their dementia, they wake up each morning as strangers, and re-enact their courtship and marriage every day. The absurdity of the situation is undercut with flashes of existential pain, reminiscent of Federico Fellini's films and Luigi Pirandello's plays. As we watch Mr. and Mrs. P overcome obstacles and fight for each other all over again every twenty-four hours, weathering infidelities, arguments, and outside interference, we see a central and essential idea emerge: that the getting and keeping of true love is perhaps the hardest work of all.

Finally, at the core of her work there is an absolute trust in the primacy of the moment, a belief in the value of capturing and bearing witness to the gifts of this world. From Cora's thrill at a hike in Colorado in "Illness at Ease" to the author herself recognizing her difficult father's true love for her in how he prepares a humble pot of spaghetti sauce, Grace's work demonstrates the conviction that, despite our losses, we can find everything we need in the world around us. We just need to see it right, as in the opening lines of "Summoning the Moment":

> The importance of saying this now
> is that it can't be said later.
>
> By then we won't remember seeing
> the crow in the trail of his cousins,
>
> or remember that, just like us,
> he has more intelligence than he needs
>
> for survival.

A FEW WORDS ON THE editing and organization of the book might be helpful. As Grace and I pored over poems and plays old and new, as well as various interviews from her radio show, we devised the following structure.

The book begins and ends with the genre she is best known for, poetry. The first section, Other Voices, showcases Grace's gift for slipping in and out of personae. It contains four sequences or suites of poems, including those in the voices of Anna Nicole Smith and Mary Wollstonecraft, as well as "Millie's Sunshine Tiki Villas" and "Cora." The fourth section, Other Lives, contains the bulk of the autobiographical poems here, ranging from her early explorations of family of origin and coming of age to the recent elegies for her husband, alongside the poems set in the Pinecrest Rest Haven.

Nestled between these two sections of poetry are selections from Grace's plays and interviews. The second section, Passionate Debates, contains excerpts from the plays *Hyena in Petticoats: The Story of Mary Wollstonecraft* and *Anna Nicole: Blond Glory*, as well as the complete text of the play *Pinecrest Rest Haven*. The third section, Memory Makers, is made up of three interviews from *The Poet and the Poem*. It was hard to choose from Grace's enormous library of conversations with contemporary masters of the craft, but I believe that the three selected—with Robert Pinsky, Lucille Clifton, and Josephine Jacobsen—display the erudition and warmth that are the hallmarks of Grace's interviewing style, as well as showcase three very different poetic sensibilities.

Bookmaking has its own kind of community, with editors, designers, proofreaders, and print consultants all collaborating to make something new and beautiful. One voice was missed in the community of *Other Voices, Other Lives*—that of Grace's late and much-beloved husband of fifty-nine years, Ken Flynn. Like Grace, Ken was a cherished friend and mentor to my husband and co-publisher, James J. Patterson and me, for many years. We were still grieving his 2013 passing when we began work on this book. One day, Grace mentioned that Ken had kept a sketchbook he called "Waiting for Grace," filled with drawings he'd made while waiting for Grace to finish a speaking engagement, a reading, an interview. Much to Grace's delight, we have incorporated two of these sketches in the book's cover design.

Now wherever this book goes, Ken will be there too, forever commemorated as the most important member of Grace's wide circle, drawn together by her fierce energy for language and love.

—Rose Solari
June 2017

Other Voices

SELECTED POEMS

Anna Nicole Smith's life was an American tragedy, managed and misused by those who filled her with drugs and propped her up to play the clown. She was a model, an aspiring actress, a contemporary Aphrodite. She died from a drug overdose at the age of thirty-nine. The following poems are excerpted from the book *Anna Nicole*.

Anna's Estate

At the ½ star hotel
the lower lip is painted bigger, to match
the dreams of being a star.
She blessed the lumpy beds, bought her own silk sheets.
This was before the moral issues, the legal issues,
the spirit of the law, the letter of the law,
the causes of death, junkies, drug addicts,
probable criminal cause, bodies exhumed,
frozen sperm, mystery sons,
living in sorrow, wrongful death,
undue influences.
Before the opalescent oceans
where she could never find the truth in things,
where she wanted a photo album so bad,
so she wouldn't die without memories—
one day, standing at the free continental breakfast
dragging her sleeve in the jelly,
someone walked by, touching her waist like a prayer,
like an enfranchisement,
and she was on her way,
in a dress made for someone much smaller,
trusting a stranger because he said,
The Good Lord can't see what happens in Hollywood.

Notes from a Distant Glacier

Interviewer: *Do you want to be someone of worth?*
Or do you want to be famous?
Designer: *If they photograph you nude,*
It's called ART.
Critic: *They should project her on the wall, the one WAAY far*
behind us.
Trainer: *In life there can be only one winner.*
Mother: *Would you please sit like a normal person?*
Manager: *Take a pill, for God's sake—any pill. Just do it.*
Doctor: *No medicine can make you stop feeling.*
Lawyer: *Don't even think about it, Anna,*
Death doesn't care about you. You owe it to the world to
make it pretty.
Director: *Give them heart, give them breast.*
Lover: *Being a blonde beauty doesn't make you a whore,*
necessarily.
Anna looks out the window.
She sees the pink azalea outside. So pretty. That color.
So perfect. It must be fake.

And Even More Than That

Anna was tired of her coloring book,
she took a big fat crayon and wrote SHIT
all over the white wall,
then the pavement outside
SHIT SHIT SHIT.
She knew now what it was to be a writer.
It felt good, cleaned out.
Maybe she could write a whole book with her red crayon.
That night she went out to dinner with the old man,
he brought his "daughter" along. He held his arm around
the dolly so tight,
Anna tried to pry his fingers off. But it was no use…
her hunger flapping like a wet towel…not his
actions that saddened, but the flat wet hand of grief
against the hot cement of her heart.
That's why she was glad she was now a writer,
insinuating herself upon the world,
having her say.

Fall Morning

Children were going to school, holding hands,
a mild morning,
the yellow rose was straining toward the sun,
God's word was spoken agreeably in the farm kitchen.
An old lady crocheted the air with her hands.
From the highest tree, a wren's sound persisted
larger than the wren,
a cigarette was thrown away in the street,
a poet walked the perimeter of the park,
the bark of the beech shone silver,
the melancholy breeze wrapped light jackets.
With the curtains drawn,
an eye mask on her face, the bottle on the floor,
Anna lies in the comfort of numbness, disabled again, thank
God, against the moment after waking, saved from all,
even the coolness of white satin sheets.
Last night on Court TV, a mother duct-taped her child's face,
to keep him from crying. But she didn't keep him from dying.

Negative Capability

Why not be happy? the counselor said.
Try to be creative, make things,
creation is a divine collaboration with God,
so why not try to do something useful? Use your hands.
Why not, thought Anna, why not?
She could start with banana bread. There were
always rotten bananas around,
and that's what it took. What a mess,
all over the kitchen, the squishing and buttery hands.
Then she ate it. Where did it go?
Where did everything always go?
She wanted to play video games
but they were too fast for her eyes and hands.
She almost wished she still played cheerleader
in the afternoon for an old man, the game where she jumped
up in the pleated skirt and yelled for his favorite team.
He said she didn't have a choice
in what he wanted to do with her,
the difference between command and management, he said.
Why not be happy,
the counselor had said to her just that morning.
If she were a loser,
like her mother always said, then where was the finder?
Who would find her? And when?
Once she heard on TV that if a man rapes you,
he steals your soul.
That had always stuck with her.
That's why she always gave in to men,
so she wouldn't have to be raped, so she could save her soul.

Undressed to Kill

She thought of all the beds she'd known—
how *now* becomes *then*—
the men with broken English,
the porno star
(a special disappointment),
some satisfying, then
unaffectionate references to
the qualities of her mind.
She remembered pillows of dismay,
unappealing bed covers,
the origins of self-doubt,
incomprehension,
purple sheets,
how many times the clock hall struck,
glimpses of a hand hurting her,
the body's study in motion,
pine needles under night sky,
milky spillage,
facts and shouts, frozen departures,
men: their capacities for worship, then hatred,
lone figures lost as if she didn't matter,
the casually curved insult,
one's self disappearing,
the bridge of mist.

Pale Slice of Moon

There was a place setting at the table
never used. Dusted and saved for
Her True Love.
What human sacrifice must be made?
How should she look when she met him?
The only way she knew how to be
was by watching soap operas on TV,
so she had servants in the background.
They came in innocent and went out with
the silver, a spent family.
Anna had to worry about their needs and who
needed her most. She sat at the long table
alone, fixed in a moment, feeling sorry for the cat.
Who would be her hero?
If someone loved you, he wouldn't hurt you.
PBS was blaring about Dante and Beatrice,
Petrarch and Laura. Who turned on that crap?
Her True Love would come with emeralds, sapphires,
and pearls. He would look into Anna's
website with her, respectfully, loving art.
Since Nature was the mouth of the heart,
Anna stuffed it with cake and waited. At night she
made noises and banged doors. That way she knew
she was alive. She could prove it.

Group Therapy

The fat therapist in a red jumpsuit asked what made each
    one happy.
Anna said a hit of coke and a shot of tequila,
then she flushed hot, everyone laughing. She thought she
    was allowed
to tell the truth...
how she lied on the manager's expense sheets,
slept with people's husbands. She thought she could
unburden the grief, but now she would shut up.
The hell with this.
Rescinda could just bring back her makeup kit
and her Vera Wang gown.
Anna stormed out.
The sign on the doctor's door: "*If you walk through Hell
you can climb your way to Paradise—Dante.*"
She would make an appointment with this Dr. Dante
and settle his hash.

Self-Improvement

Anna Nicole would break her own mold,
no one else could do it.
She wanted to get to the bottom of something
besides a bottle.
Her stomach tightened when
Alpha Pros tried to help her personality disorder.
She had a problem but it was
HER problem. HERS. Something to have and to hold.
The adhesions to life still hurt. Now,
she was supposed to act dumb. The
hardest part was to act. She was dumb.
Why make it art? She was confused.
The waiter said, just yesterday: You are well known
What's your name again?
Maybe the Walk of Fame wasn't all that much.
She told herself there was work to do, learn the ABCs of life,
words that matched, keep a journal, play hide and seek
with destiny, not push it. She spoke to herself sternly once.
If only she had listened.

Joytown

At the edge of thought, a frozen pond melted.
The Guy in armor had taken it all off, and was
sitting on the floor sobbing.
Anna never saw such a thing. She should run...
tell him she was expected somewhere...or...
someone was waiting...she needed to be alone...
This strapping brute of a man had suddenly
become a minute creature, shaking with shame.
Anna knew she needed imagination for this one,
but trained otherwise from birth,
never had a chance.
She tried to look serious. She tried to look
dignified, but the naked man on the floor
reduced her to simplicity.
Could she name the problem?
Name her darkness?
The side of her sleeve was offered to his running nose.
Her field of vision blurred.
He told her this was his first day on the job
and he couldn't go through with it.
He was a PhD student working his way through anthropology.
She bent down and took his head and arms.
Now what would she do with her unused understanding.
There under the bed, she saw her other satin slipper.
Somehow she knew it would fit.

Where Love Is Meant to Be

The gardener told Anna Nicole he could build
a small temple
where the compost was once housed, now removed,
as nothing would grow on that hard earth anyway.
Anna said yes. She would like a small shrine of her own.
Something bright and shiny
with a little cement on the ground
with a gold star in it with her name.
She was not the best businesswoman, having failed typing,
but she could even charge admission.
Public access was ruefully discouraged by the guards
(close friends excepted, like the press).
Anna would be kind to herself
and mount only those photos
with men who did not humiliate her, also some animals she
        rescued.
Or just the animals.
When she was little and too scared to talk,
she held out a hamster in her hands, so people would relate.
There would be pictures of school supplies,
and Psalm 17 could be projected on the wall
about singing a song anew.
Then the idea of singing lessons came up
and she had a good feeling about that. She wanted so much
to write a song about *why what they did to her did not kill her.*
But she would have to figure out **why**, first.

The next set of poems, from *What I Would Do for Love*, is written in the voice of the groundbreaking eighteenth-century feminist writer Mary Wollstonecraft. Her famous *A Vindication of the Rights of Woman* instructed women to seek their equality. Mary's conflict lay in the fact that while she fought for equality with male intellectuals, she also wanted their love. She found happiness in marriage to the philosopher William Godwin. She died at thirty-eight, of complications from giving birth to their second child, also named Mary, who would later wed the poet Percy Bysshe Shelley and write the novel *Frankenstein*.

I Can Think of Far Worse Things

Than to be a governess—
Saying "that's that" and hustling children
To the bath—
Oh yes, far worse things…
Like prostitution, for example,
Or embroidering, for that matter…
Or marrying someone I do not love.
And although I've never had the pox,
And one eyelid droops a little,
I am not ugly. If I lack sparkle
It's just because
There's such a narrow light in this room.
Do people think I should be a squirrel or a rabbit?
In the shed eating wood? Unworthy of my work?
No, with twelve guineas saved
One could start her own school,
Or buy some self-respect,
Or even start a dowry.
If I have to work for people whose
Fortune was not made in this lifetime,
Then I will tend to them sweetly,
Saving this beautiful handwriting for night.

Dear Reverend Clare

You ask if hope gets me up in the morning,
I say yes,
Not in your house where
Everything exists,
But in mine
Where all things are lost.
The top latch takes the weight of the door,
And so it is true, as I teach
Liza and Everina all that you teach me.
You say my child's sense of wonder is coupled with
A grown person's knowing grief,
And why shouldn't it be?
You are talking to a girl with a pencil hidden
In a broken cup
On top the highest shelf
Stained by curdled cream
Behind a ceramic pitcher
Where it cannot be thrown away.

Lady Kingsborough Hates Me

For reading my *Mary, A Fiction*
Aloud.
She said I was a mouse in a big house
Trying to become a lion, turning
Her children against her.

Today
She called me "Bitter little angry little sullen little..."
And said I'd never be named "Mrs."

My writing
Thoughts on the Education of Daughters
Angered her further.
I can hear her bleating still:
"Really now. A masculine mind, Mary?
A governess with a man's mind?"
She said
I killed love,
And pointed to the tree
Her yardman had strangled with rope.
The tree outgrew its hold, she said. It choked.
I read
Original Stories to the children.
How dare I write that parents
Should raise their own children
Instead of servants.
　　　　Coming away
I feel guilt for being light of heart.
No one else but myself to care for.

Am I Afraid to Be a Woman of Significance?

The fear of blindness is worse
Than the fact.
Rousseau ridicules us,
"Educate women and the more they
Resemble our sex, the less power will
They have over us."

Power over them is not what I seek, but power over ourselves!

We are like little cucumbers
Row upon row, gleaming,
Ready to be cut, sugared, or baked.

The moral life is to see
The harvest! The peeling,
Be the knife! The self as source.
London. With a job of my own
In a flat with old walls,
I get up earlier than most men.
I write. All day I write for other people.

Do our dreams affect our days, or
Do our days affect our dreams...
I would like someone waiting for me.

I long for a cup of tea.
The light is on the wall.
It falls on my plain wooden bed,
The gray curtain.

Teach yourself how to think, Mary!
For no one else will do it for you.
Be the knife.

Mr. Johnson

"Uncommon Kindness" is what I call you
Instead of "publisher."
Telling me I am "the first of a new genus!"
I tremble at the attempt.
We must not, on any account,
Inform my brother or father
For ridicule has always been the unfriendliest advice.

The October winds blow through London yet
I hear only words exhorting my mission.
I must be independent!
When a writer writes
The words are taken by the reader
But they always belong to the writer.

This body

An unwilling recipient for spirit
Finally fills
With the breath of confidence
Because of you.

My luck is changing
Today I stubbed my toe
And to the breaking said:
Thank you life. I feel something besides terror.

I have a body, a mind, a heart.
I invite the world to lay its head on my stomach and listen.

Dead Cod in the Sun

Gilbert, again and again, Gilbert
Again and again. You leave me for fantasy.
Every woman is an idea you come to life for.
When we dine you look over my shoulder. When
We shop you compliment the
Shop girl's throat-piece pretending
It would be good for me.
As you dance with another
You talk of my brilliance, my genius, Gilbert,
You keep talking about me
So your partner cannot move away, and after
She will say, *He loves Mary so much*
He did nothing but talk of her as he held
Me close. He must love
Her very much, for he leaned against me many times
To say her name.
I, a woman of words, freeze when I try to tell you this aloud.

Even Death Does Not Want Me

Three weeks in bed,
I cannot even plan
A suicide well it seems.
Dear Diary, you are
All I have. Liza and Everina
Suffer because of my act,
A death gone wrong,
Leaving me this life
As cold as the water.
I remember the lifting.
I closed my eyes and
Felt the sweet sweep,
A swirling of relief and then the noise,
The lights, the clamor, cold
Cobblestones
People in a circle looking down.
The bright lanterns,
A rough blanket,
A loud voice in my ear,
"Ain't that funny. It was her skirts
What saved her, billowing up around her arse."
And then a woman,
"Now she'll think twice of wearing pants."

Overheard Today

A vicious sound,
"Famous lady with her book
Telling us how to act..."

I could not hear the rest,
And leaned in closer
To the murmuring,

Until she straightened.
And then I saw she spoke of me!
Mary Wollstonecraft.
She held my book

"*Vindication...*"
And shook it at her partner.
My face flushed.

Were it a man speaking
I would not crumble
But now I fear my dream

Is uninhabitable.
All women are in danger
Unless we pick the

Bough from the trees ourselves
Yet a stranger was condemning me
In a public place

Why not grant me
The courtesy given male authors, saying
"It is controversial"—

Her fury ascends in my body
She said I made her quest for survival
All the worse!

Because I can read and write?
Does that give me a masculine mind?
Or just a mind?

I Love You, Mr. Godwin

It was rare in the extreme
To find the kind of writing person
I wanted to live with,
The kind of writing person
For whom loving was ill advised yet,
Here I am in your abode,
I am the Mary whose prayers are answered,
I am the Mary where the death of my mind's eye
Could not stop the beating of my heart,
I didn't want to lie fearful forever,
I wanted to polish my boots,
And comb their tassels,
Before putting them on to die,
The world had forgot
That women had thoughts worth hearing,
And so the thoughts they had,
Forget to be heard!
Until tonight,
William, William, William Godwin,
I kiss you on top of your big nose.

This Meeting we are having, what shall we call it?
A dream we are having together?

Diary Notes

Cities and boats disappear, replaced by my faithful diary.
It holds true rage (Can rage not be true?),
The consequences of pride,
The rapid affections that fly by, my dark apprehensions
The streets of torment disappear when I write.
Leaves of humiliation flower, turn from tight rude buds,
To fill vast spaces.

For William Godwin

I would cook with berry juice until
Our clothes were red,
Roast a lamb in the fire,
Carve meat for our empty purses,
Climb the yellow tree with skirts pulled up,
Sit above London singing my William throat.
The candles will burn in all rooms all day all summer,
I will learn to sew,
I will walk backwards until you come home,
I will wear your garters, shine your keys, fold
Your papers for all the world to see.
And windowsills too,
I will perch there in motion with rain in my hair and the taste
Of cider as sincere
As the dark you will come through.

*T*he following poems are excerpted from *Millie's Sunshine Tiki Villas*, a novella in verse set in an eponymous retirement community. The residents of the community—Muriel, Lady Veronica, Harry, Harry's wife, Triumph, and Conrad—clash and compete against each other in search of romance and revenge. The characters Coco and Muriel are also minor characters in the poems and play set at Pinecrest Rest Haven.

Millie's Sunshine Tiki Villas

Nobody remembers Millie. No one knows why the Seniors'
Residence was in her name. Some believe she must have been
a show girl because of the antique bar in the craft house
displaying a picture of a flapper with yellow curls and a bit
of a knee. Some claim to have known Millie but when questioned,
fade off to blurred memory. It's still unclear if she imagined
the resort cottages as homes for retired actors, or senior citizens,
what with the decor of showbiz and the indoor/outdoor stages
at either end of the complex. Who knew of its beginnings, this
semicircular grouping of beach houses with thatched fake grass roofs
which flew up and down with each breeze, and who could have
foreseen the future occupants—("Elders Only" dictated the by-laws)
who'd come to spend their final days amidst imitation Hawaiian
grandeur. The plastic volcano once went down into the swimming
pool, then it sported a bar along the top crag (with barbecues at its rupture),
now all gone, all dormant, fires out, pool emptied, and a world of seniors
taking their air along the painted paths.

It is thrilling to think of the day Coco and Muriel saw Lady V
move in, deciding they should bring a welcome wagon.
What a pleasure to think of it. Coco in her caftan with penguin
designs, Muriel wearing a penguin lounging suit. Lady Veronica
said nothing at all of their rivalries, due to the fact she was royalty.
But she must have been irked by what she saw in these two
trespassers although she kept her own counsel, or at least tried.
She dolefully heated the electric kettle as if whatever were
imprisoned could finally be free. Her home, Lady vowed
secretly, would be, after this, unfrequented and she, for one,
could not wait. Coco and Muriel continued with the outer crust
of brightness shared, verbally dancing as if there were a knife
in the heart which could be worked loose. Coco made sure Lady V
knew the dates of the Kulture Circle. This week there would
be poetry where all "nabbed remembrances of childhood" were
welcome. Muriel helped herself to a gorgeous slice of rhubarb tart
and added that Coco was bungling the business again.
The Kulture Circle was really honoring poetic prose about
"a world changing which was not really changing." Apparently
each had worked on next week's poetry agenda without benefit
of mutual agreement, but there was anger in the air
as Muriel swore she had the correct theme.

A bowl of roses, a solitary dinner, this is all Conrad wished for in life.
It wasn't his drinking the people didn't like, it was his personality
when he drank. The hell with them. To hell with all the stupid
residents of the Sunshine Villas. He'd buy, cook, and eat at his
own pace. He appeared to be a benign, tall, slightly stooped,
gentle-hearted man, and, although their affections were not
returned, most women loved Conrad. Each woman seemed
to find something about themselves they liked in Connie.
He'd give a waiter a two-dollar tip, even for dining,
and tell how well the Help picked up the dishes. How lovely
he could be, thought the occasional woman companion.
There was no solicitude, in turn, toward the women from Conrad,
for he rather disliked the lot but could hardly bring himself
to tell them so. He just got nicer and nicer. Thus Conrad
was looked for at every Sunshine party and, hot with their wiles,
women waited for him to find them, which he never did.
In this way a quaint nostalgia grew around the elderly
man about that which is and that which was not, the same quality
perhaps seen differently by each seer.

From the everlasting sleep of human confusion, Muriel
was sure that Conrad loved her. Muriel felt it the moment
she met him. And after Coco left her each day at four, Muriel
would stop by to see if Connie wanted dinner. He never did,
we already described his eating style, but on this particular day
Muriel outfoxed the Conrad man and brought her favorite dish
with her. She didn't warn him of this cooking triumph.
It was "Tuna Olé" and once she'd won a contest with it,
with two prizes, a trip for two to Mexico (which she never took)
and a blue and yellow casserole dish (hand painted) which she did.
Up to the door she came. Conrad looked and he almost got away
but for his shadow which she must have seen crouched behind
the door. The door flung open (he must remember to buy a lock)
and there she was looking straight at him as if he were the last man
left after the bomb had exploded. He looked shaken.
She beamed as if she were about to set off a wonderful memory
all of her own, "I brought you a surprise."

Lady Veronica thought if she could enter Harry's room at midnight,
or even get as far as this screened-in porch, that would do. If she
could listen to him snore, she could get the final ingredient for
her concoction. The aural part. She'd have to use an old warthog
tusk to stir, but the auditory was absolutely impossible to substitute
with any other ingredient for the plan. It mattered (even less as she
grew old) whether anyone loved another or not. But Harry's Wife
with her yellow watery eyes touched something in Veronica's own past.
Lady Veronica remembered a cat she owned once during World War II,
a fluffy creature which was blown away in her own neighborhood
in London. It was the only friend the wartime girl could have, and
so she even shared her own rationed foodstuffs with the animal.
Veronica had long since forgotten a loss of any pet, oh yes,
she'd written the requisite dead pet poems when in college
but time is exactly what they say, a cleanser of wounds.
Harry's wife, and her dead cat; There was something similar there.
The timid wife…her pet animal… Whatever the reason,
Veronica felt she could help, perhaps just this once
before she retired her considerable gifts.

Muriel lifted the paper carefully out of the typewriter.
Her page had looked so much prettier penned in hand, cursive writing,
her forte, but no publisher (she knew) would evaluate the work unless
it were professional. She read the words quietly to herself. Her memoirs
were finally begun. It took a broken ankle to direct her toward
her glorious journey to the self.
I was born unawares (margin note: unaware?) clean and happy
and in favor of racial equality (note: too early to bring in societal concerns?).
My mother used to dangle a yellow rubber glove in front of me.
To this day I love yellow. Not the bright yellow as in the daffodils'
daring dexterity but more the muted glistening soft synthetic yellow
one finds in morning's first light (are those two last words plagiary?).
The maid would put her cheek next to mine and she smelled of soap.
I miss her so much (comment on her being black?). I had not yet met
Coco who would usurp my life and call it hers (giving away the
plot too soon?) (excise). Years later I would own many a diamond ring
and will have won an award from the Wendy Ward Show
as the best mistress of events at the Montgomery Ward's fashion show
for children under eight.

Triumph was well named. He had a theory that people lived up
to the name they were given (or gave themselves), for instance,
for a time he called himself "Rich," and then "Ample," but
suddenly one day he announced his name was TRIUMPH.
The men all winked and wanted to hear of the exploits but it
was personal power of which he spoke and from that moment on,
he steadily built his stature and physical ability to that of a very
strong sixty-year-old. On Sunday afternoons he gave exhaustive
talks at the South dining room (small unairconditioned
but good acoustics) on motivation and self-approbation.
Many a man who was wheeled in or struggled on a walker
tried to leave "without crutches." They fell, of course,
but they tried. And that was his message. He once gave a talk
entitled "Flying" in which he proffered that if one had enough
faith in himself—really enough faith—a true belief—in, say,
jumping from the window—that man could FLY. But it would take
an unaltered belief in one's self and a true unblemished understanding
that thought creates action.

Muriel moved gracefully in the twilight, touching the golden leaves
with her ironwood walking cane, past the dining hall with its late
kitchen workers, through the magic forest of faux pine, onto the hill
to Conrad's outer villa. She'd already forgiven him, poor dear, for
his misguided and unsuccessful attempt at defiling her. Oh men
were so naughty. How could she hold his indiscretion against
him for long. Such a lovely gentleman. Soft-spoken, anxious to please,
refined, modest, and shy. What if in a moment of passion,
with unanticipated ecstasy, he nearly violated the flower of their
relationship. Not his fault. Man was but a biological impulse
(she'd read somewhere). And, if it must be known, Muriel saw
a neat fitting of this within her memoir. Saving the best for last,
she chuckled. Although in her heart hoped that the life's last chapter
wasn't written about the wily Conrad and the arduous Muriel.
Ascending the grassy plane, she had a heightened view of Conrad's
sweet villa, one of the three-story kind, top of the line, most expensive.
She sighed. He was a man of taste, leading the expansive life.
Lights out below. Hmmm. This was early for retirement and
it was barely past the end of the day. Perhaps Connie was in his study,
holding a leather-bound book of Bartlett's famous quotations,
ostrich-binding of some sort of bibliophile like him.

There was a rustling down the stairs of taffeta and lace and then,
looking up from his supine position, Triumph saw Conrad
standing over him, a face filled with fear and confusion—
Conrad the ballgown of pink moiré with a small shoulder
stole of slightly ratty white rabbit. He'd lost an earring rushing
down the stairs and Triumph leaped up—taking both of Connie's
wrinkled hands in his own, and like Titania from a dream,
declared his everlasting love.
Let us be clear that Conrad liked the feel of ladies' frocks
but had no intention of going further in them. The absence of all
desire had left him interested only in fabric and texture;
and who is to say we should do otherwise? Would it be more valuable
to pass his midnight hours sweeping leaves from the gutters of
human contact? Or wrapped in the magic of chiffon and peau de soie?

Safely at home, Muriel opened the folder. She lay upon the pink
chintz chaise and took a deep breath, expectantly. Scanning quickly,
Ha! Where was the lilt of language here. Declarative sentences
starting with the date of Coco's birth! And here her birthweight
and first words. Hmmm. This was somewhat similar to Muriel's
wonderful work in the beginning, the heartfelt reminiscence,
the color yellow, but one could not be sure, and still
could never sue for plagiary because the words weren't
in the same order and you cannot copyright an idea. This,
Muriel had read in one of the authors' journals she had sent to her
from England. The British were so much more advanced,
so much more cultured. Muriel's heart stopped in midsentence.
There, in large block print was a jeering line—DEAR MURIEL,
I KNOW AT THIS MOMENT YOU'RE READING THIS
AND I HAVE MY TRUE MEMOIRS
UNDER LOCK AND KEY FOREVER MORE.
HA HA. YOUR FRIEND, COCO.

"*Cora*" is a suite of poems styled after William Carlos Williams's improvisations *Kora in Hell*. This present-day Cora is a waitress in the Golden Glow Café; she's in love with Charlie who, unfortunately, is already married to Dorothy.

My Boss Thinks I'm Great

Charlie, you always want to go
just when the cat is sleeping
on my feet. You always have
some place to go. Charlie, you
always have to leave saying
you have to paint the trim. A
mistress doesn't need to be
first and foremost but you
always want to leave. All the
muscles in my stomach have been
removed and put back in place.
I use Garden Joy. My legs under
the cat are smooth. Smooth. You're
just like the girls at work. They
steal my counter rags, then they
leave to go home. I never have
anything to mop up with. They
always say they don't steal the
counter rags. But they do. Merv
Griffin, I have a secret. I've
always thought of you when Charlie
screws me. Where do you always
go, Merv?

Weary of magic glasses?
sitting in meditation, vague
accumulations of pain
cries in the eyes of children
How it is to be left alone

With Equal Felicity

In each case the central character
is introduced in the objective
biographical manner against the
sheets, compared as a statement
to that bed restricted by curiosity
and surprise and suspense the
naked man approaches. Let it be
said that splendor and terror are
one, that the night table with
the dead plant is attributed to
the light of blue shade. The
marginal aspects of love are
simple organisms. They are
intentions, techniques, and the
business at hand, the tea tray,
the swollen uterus, the persuasion
of great happiness, the roar
against the sky, the decrepit old
woman, the thin air, the feathering
of bones outside when, like petals,
all is quiet.

There is a tale told that things are
     related to us all
   and soon
Soon we will spring to it

Cora
An American Beauty
Rose

The tit cuts across the page
and stops. What can I tell you
about this. The tit rises.
Three men on a ladder poke it
into place. They cut into it
with knives. They put their fingers
behind the mammary glands. They
stuff a jellyfish in but not
with scissors. Nothing so mean
as that. It consumes the house.
The nipple flaccid floating on
the krispies. Lift it high. Pass
the salt. The tip of this pen
is actually the tit which is
human. You're a marvel, he says,
as he eats it with a fork.

A musical silence
Unreasonably sweetening the
                gathering air, only
        the locusts join up
                        oh baby
Follow the follow   *intervene*
        the flinty facts
                        overcome
                our isolation

Organ World

Cora just washed her hair.
She could still feel the heat
coming off her. She says to
Charlie, "Will you marry me."
Charlie says, "I'm already
married." Cora says, "I didn't
ask you your problems." This
eccentric and unusual behavior
suggests an unsound mind. It is
unrealistic to believe Cora will
abandon her needs or that she
should not have needs. "I want
to look my best," Cora said, and
in their way, they separated
to make ready for love. She
turned out the bedroom light.
She stroked herself. "When he
sees the damn thing in the light
he doesn't want it." This is the
holding pattern. Then the need
floats. It goes down under the
rabbit hutch, on down further,
beyond the cabbage patch, the grapes
on the vine, the seed under us all.
The stick catches it and flowers
lilies. He opens the bathroom door.
"Hi Toots."

Arms lifted into the blue air
    as cold as the last white star you will see
    one moment before meeting it midway
    or imagining its kiss

She Says

It's my birthday
Charlie says   What do you want
        Anything
Charlie says   What do you need
        Anything
You want a great big party?
        No
Well then what *do*
you want?
        A present
How am I supposed to know what
you need?
        Anything
You have use of all the facilities
here.
        She leaves. He leaves.

To honor and love are verbs
Of accountability
                I do not signify them
        on such a broad basis, reducing
                their qualities
But there are explicit things one can do

There Is No Heat in This House

Charlie—Button-Eyes, how come you
don't look back when your wife is
home and I am here. Me—Your Cora—
either place you turn around like
we are two bad choices. I have the
patience of Job. I am a patient
woman. In the supermarket I don't
change lines when the cash register
is broke. I wait. Me, the Puerto
Ricans, the blacks, and one Chinese,
we didn't change lines when every
body else gave up. The conveyor
belt was broken—after all—this kid
picks out a round ceramic flute from
his pocket right there. What a
wonderful sound. In front of the Cocoa
Puffs—like far away—as if there was
a light all covered with snow you
could almost see. An old guy patted
his woman's back. I thought, look how
nice he treats her. It must be his
second wife. Charlie, you are smart
in some respects but dumb everywhere
else. Possibilities you are dumb about.

What it would be like if you'd turn
around. You only know what is actually
happening—not what could happen.
Consider dreaming of me when you are
with her and vice-versa. It's a
beginning.

Or why he ever had his nights
        the ceremonies which were lost
    the memories
                which did not have him
All the old laws spilling from our aprons

When Was the Last Time You Got a Present

When was the last time you got a present
(you the greatest thing since sliced cheese)
a cozy knit scarf
with airy macrame braid,
nostalgic little school desk
which keeps memo pad handy,
a light and lacy slumber bra,
your very own painting set,
full circle brush
which styles glamorous coiffures,
a chord piano to play
in ten days,
a ballpoint pen that writes
in twelve colors,
garden of gourmet herbs in a
hanging strawberry pot,
a sewing machine that fits in your palm,
the charm of crewel embroidery. (You
the greatest thing since whipped cream.)
They have definitely polluted your well,
kid. What about charming calendar towels
featuring lovely scenes, or a fiery
man-made opal.

In my famous brand
            waltz gown
The fortunes of due processes
Are as imponderable as ever
      foreshadowing all which is
   palpable

All rendered us
in our
nonrun problemless pantyhose

Dorothy,

When you showed off what if
I didn't clap, says the man.
What if I didn't appreciate
Ireland, boycott lettuce,
go on outings, pick up pebbles,
pedestal-watch-you, kill off
possibilities, look at your
goddamn pure white bird on
a rock in the pictures? These
are promising ideas. Consider
my not liking it. And also—
your friend Norma Blue runs
like a horse.

          Love,
            Charlie

Cora's Night School

What ways are you depressed what
ways were you depressed what
situations caused you to feel
depressed what was your reaction
to the situation how realistic
about the situation were you if
you were realistic you would
only be disappointed. Disappointment.
What ways were you disappointed.
What situations caused you to feel
disappointed. What were your reactions
to these situations. How was your
sense of reality more realistic.
How were you (are you) depressed
about writing about the wish motif
or disappointed. Begin writing, class,
about how realistic you are. Begin
writing.

As if pages were
                    never counted
        in the dark
Disperse
The spirit from the broom,
                    and bread
Autonomy dies
            from whose dream
                        it was

Dorothy Counts Plastic Lemons

I speak of broken toilets.
We plan around the wall in
the kitchenette, a wall which
can come down walking us right
out, then, to the swimming pool
which could have an inflatable
top and provide warmth in the
winter or we could go to San
Martin where there are peach
trees, late coffee in the morning,
The New York Times available in
the same building, and meetings
together at lunchtime, late to
go, early to return. Charlie and I
speak of broken toilets, we plan
to wallpaper, there is talk of
indoor-outdoor carpet so ugly, we
can cover it up.

Like hermits against
        a backdrop or rock
Conquering dilemmas
                with the beautiful
Lies engaged in
        when dealing with gorillas

Illness at Ease

Dorothy's wig. Cora could see it
from behind the counter. Dorothy
walking by the window. And a
white hearse going by behind her.
Dropping to her knees, Cora's
head only reached as high as the
spigot on the coffeemaker. She
prayed, craving the benevolent
healer to make the shine come
back to her hair. She rose
restored. Crashings in the
kitchen. Bashing. Something
broken. Not all angry gods are
just ones, Cora wiping the french
fry bin, patterns of grease in
the sign of the cross now a
circle, wiping eternally. Cora
heard the juke. Music she couldn't
dance to if she tried. Freshened
by prayer, Cora had the familiar
feeling she would live forever and
even after that, she would never
have to die. Saved from eternity
again. By a see-through glass. A
wonderful thing in front of
a diner. She felt the same thrill
once while descending four thousand
feet in eight miles at Wolfcreek
Pass, Colorado.

Where are the inevitable conclusions
        promised
The premise to our goals?
And why not now
                kissing our gold tooth, they do
                whenever they catch our smile.

Eating Gardenias

Making plans to leave, eating
crackers and butter: Dear
Charlie, I wanted to be the
first to tell you I don't love
you anymore. Click click click.
The green arrow that glistens GO
stops. The cat chases a fly. Silly
cats, they have their drawbacks.
He catches it. Oh Cora, Cora, where
is your self-respect. And why when I
say that do you cry? A tree floats
past the window. "Uh huh." What did
you learn, Cora, dancing in a dress
with rhinestone straps across your
back: Dear Charlie, I only exist if
you watch me. Cora throws a rock at
the cat's feet. Dances. Charlie killed
a dog once. Bashed its head in for
attacking a rooster. He was living

in New Mexico at the time. He then
ate the rooster which was still alive.
He killed it first though. Cora falls
asleep. "Oh." The pen, the phone, all
one. She walks down the street with a
gown flowing and the wind blowing
through her arms. Everyone is cheering.

And the hill stays
And the red
       commutes
             the sun
To the hill
From the leaf,
         which had its tree
Now the ground
            found
Though the newest on any branch
Although the reddest

Out in Numbers

Out in numbers, the birds, Dorothy noted.
Charlie tells her to fork over the toast.
Dorothy remains lonely enough to answer
the phone after, looking at her veins,
the blood clots fade. Charlie believes
the Chinese put mice in their food. His
divine act of rebellion—never eating
any. That night they made love with their
mouths like desexed cats. The only weapon
where—in the name of the law—you can
kill yourself singing three blind mice.
Charlie is deeply affected by all he sees
and does. Dorothy is used to the inconvenience.

When reading the map
And there are no more delusions left
              it is time to set up signals
Equalizing ecstasy and groans
Here,
       an eye
              here,
                 a tear

Cora, Aware of a Mystery

A wide wide street with greenery, a
sun in the morning, he would go to
work and come home, he would come
home to eat dinner, a small roast
perhaps, some green vegetables. He
would not try to talk in the deep voice
because she would already believe him.
Wednesday, Thursday, Friday, the walk
where there are flowers of every
variety. No one else to please. A room
under the stairs. An inner place, the
roof in an ascending line, the heart-
shaped cat. Two goldfish on our side
of the room not fatally wounded.

What is it if you have
                        a beauty mark
          curl
     soft soles of feet
               scarcely used
          hands
       a pink unscratched tongue
     upturned breasts
Legs, strong but not too muscular

Business Is Slow

Nothing left to play. Charlie could
beat any man at checkers. He gave away
his card set out of the goodness of
his heart to a bum who wanted some
free food. Charlie felt a rising in
his crotch and a thickening. He thought
of Cora—dumb, couldn't live without
him. Dorothy, crocodile. Blunderers.
He didn't want none. Both alike. They
should meet. They should. They should
meet. What if. He could get them to be
friends. What could anybody prove.
Customers were all stupid, spilling ketchup,
arguing about change, all the time complaints
in the Golden Glow Café. Even the fancy
places he managed. The same type customers.

The holding back of pleasures
Is getting better than possible
      especially your annunciations
Coming strong
Ascending toward the sky
Whimpering   hello   goodbye
      watching everything begin and end
from a distance

Some Plain Talk About Shoplifting

The man in the cardigan sweater
is a law breaker. But O I can't
complain—Ah he entered my room
by the window, by the window.
Entered my. By the window. His
black briefcase was half full.
Are you listening? Or do I have
to keep talking. I am trying to
tell you something. Simply. There
are law breakers everywhere we can't
complain about. What do you know of
love? As for me, I always think it
will be better than it is.

✥

Goodbye

Charlie, you just don't
occur to me

Cora

Passionate Debates

PLAYS

Hyena in Petticoats: The Story of Mary Wollstonecraft

(excerpt)

CHARACTERS

MARY WOLLSTONECRAFT: Seventeen, ages to her thirties during play; strong manipulative, aggressive, argumentative; moves to vulnerable

EVERINA: Mary's younger sister; stoic, dry, sensible, angry; moves to compassion

LIZA: Mary's youngest sister; elflike, vacant, capricious, nervous, silly; moves to strength and resolve

REVEREND CLARE: Middle-aged

GILBERT IMLAY: American, thirties

JOSEPH JOHNSON: Middle-aged

WILLIAM GODWIN: Thirties

PUNCH

JUDY

LADY KINGSBOROUGH: Voiceover

SETTING

TIME: Eighteenth-century England (1776–97)

PLACE: Epping and London

PROLOGUE

PUNCH and JUDY emerge from opposite sides of the stage. They sometimes do tricks, and mime their words. They sometimes address each other as characters, and sometimes the audience as narrators. They cartwheel on and bow to the audience.

PUNCH: I am Punch.

JUDY: And I am Judy.

PUNCH: History is our role and duty.

JUDY: Today we have a story to mend.
        Mary Wollstonecraft seeks equality with men.

PUNCH: We show the foolishness of women again.

(JUDY steps on his foot.)

JUDY: She was born 1759, one of seven, second in line.

PUNCH: Mary is the baby's name.

JUDY: Mary wanted power and fame.

PUNCH: Her father, a farmer who beat her mother.

JUDY: And cruel to his daughter above all other.
        She wrote books both brave and true.

PUNCH: She muddled women's minds like stew.

JUDY: If you met her you wouldn't stay true!

(She bops him.)

PUNCH: The American Revolution.
        The French Revolution.

JUDY: *(Jumps up and down.)* The vindication of women! Evolution!

PUNCH: Ha! Books do not change anything.

JUDY: Then neither does man, church, or sin!

PUNCH: What do women hope to do?

JUDY: Change your minds, your ideas too!

PUNCH: No woman was ever minister.

JUDY: Too busy serving and saying SIR.

PUNCH: No woman was a first-rate fighter.

JUDY: Now they'll fight as first-rate writers.

PUNCH: I am going back inside. *(Drops out of sight.)*

JUDY: There is nowhere you can hide.

PUNCH: *(Offstage.)* The circus comes to London town.

JUDY: Mary Wollstonecraft seeks renown.

SCENE 5

MARY and CLARE are seated at the table.

MARY: And why do you continue to help me, Reverend Clare? I can never repay you.

CLARE: Nothing gives a man more pleasure than to save a young lady who could not otherwise be saved.

MARY: *(Unbelieving.)* Save a young lady?

CLARE: You, my dear, you were but a tiny worm in a cocoon and now look at you. You are learning to fly.

MARY: Oh, yes. Fly.

CLARE: A man gets great pleasure in breaking open that cocoon for a young woman, a beauteous one at that.

MARY: Excuse me Reverend Clare, I owe you much and love you more than a little, but—does not a cocoon open on its own?

CLARE: With much more difficulty, my dear, much much more difficulty.

MARY: Only the butterfly knows how it feels to be free. You cannot do that for me.

CLARE: True, true. But I can teach freedom.

MARY: But you cannot know freedom.

CLARE: Whatever do you mean?

MARY: Only that you cannot know freedom unless you have known what it is *not* to be free.

CLARE: We will save that for a logic lesson at a later time.

MARY: I think about the way I started to read, a sweet code broken, hieroglyphics curling upward. I saw them as letters shaped like petals rising upward. I remember when I was very small wondering when words upon the page would bloom. I thought they were living things.

CLARE: Writing was just the next step after thinking, Mary, and you did that well. Yet I must admonish you.

MARY: But I have always honored all you said.

CLARE: It is difficult for you to give me the credit due for creating you. Without my help, you would still be content polishing kettles and sweeping floors.

MARY: I would not! The door I opened with all my might, my *own* might, you wish to close for me?

CLARE: I gave you the key to the door, Mary. The next lesson learned for you, Mary Wollstonecraft, will be modesty and humility.

MARY: And what of dignity, Reverend Clare?

CLARE: We shall save that for a discussion on deductive reasoning, our next meeting. *(He exits.)*

MARY: *(Reads as she starts to write. Begins reverently.)* Dear Reverend Clare, son, husband, teacher, what shall I call you then—teaching me clarity, a growing understanding of how words are made, why we wish to be heard, how we bridge to other people's minds. *(Suddenly she changes her mood, throws her writing board down, and stands upon it.)* But what we are worth? And in whose eyes? You cannot do that for me.

INTERLUDE

LIZA: *(To audience.)* I asked Mary how she learned so much. She said she did it by herself while the Reverend was speaking. In the months that followed, Mary taught us all she knew and will continue our learning when she returns. But now she leaves us. I am frightened without her. I bought her a gift with my savings… it is used, but it is clean.

SCENE 6

EVERINA is working at the table. MARY enters.

MARY: Everina! Where is it?

EVERINA: Mary, my hands are filled with flour.

MARY: My packet of papers.

EVERINA: What now, Queen Mary. What distress do we have now?

MARY: My papers. They were right there. I left them here. You saw them, I know.

EVERINA: Mary, I had to clear this table to make the bread.

MARY: This is more my table than yours!! Did I not make its legs when Father broke down the door? Isn't this what I made of a broken door? My table more than anyone's. Where are my writings?

EVERINA: What is it this family needs? Bread or scribblings?

MARY: Tell me or I swear I'll— *(Grabs the dough and threatens her with it.)*

EVERINA: In the fire, Mary. You lack humility. You are not the only one living in this house.

(MARY runs to the fireplace. LIZA enters with arm full of papers.)

LIZA: I reached in, Mary. I think you have them all. But a little ruined on the edge.

MARY: *(Exasperation near collapse.)* Three years in the making, Everina. Three years in this madhouse, at night lying in front of Mother's door to save her! Father's drunken rages. Ned's ridicule. Everina. Are you crazy? Ruining my work?

LIZA: I found them for you Mary.

MARY: I leave for Ireland. This is a fine goodbye.

EVERINA: You are getting out of this house, Mary. More than we can hope for.

MARY: To one just like it. Governess for Lady Kingsborough.

LIZA: I found them for you Mary. If you leave, I am afraid.

MARY: *(Softening.)* Listen, sisters. When we three were small, we were like one. Come.

(They hold their right hands together.)

MARY: *(Reluctantly.)* Who hurts one, hurts all. Together we stand, apart we fail.

EVERINA AND LIZA: We three are one.

MARY: *(Pulls her hand away.)* Liza, Everina, if it is true, we are one, are you the part of me that hates myself? Why is it when I tell you my fears, you beg me to do what others want?

EVERINA: Why do you take your poor disposition and sour life out on the ones who love you, your own sisters? You will always get what you wish, Mary. So leave us then.

LIZA: Let us not argue, please. I found the papers.

MARY: *(Puts papers in her carryall.)* I will write you soon.

LIZA: No, save your beautiful handwriting for your stories.

EVERINA: Don't forget your promise. After this. Our school, Mary. Don't forget.

MARY: As soon as I save twelve guineas, we begin.

LIZA: The empty house at Newington Green. A school for girls. I'll help you Mary.

EVERINA: I'll believe it when the cock lays eggs. Mary lives in the land of possibilities and broken promises.

LIZA: Be nice, Everina. Mary leaves us.

EVERINA: I want to, but Mary acts such the perfect ass.

MARY: No one is perfect. Tend to your logic, Everina.

LIZA: Wait, Mary. *(Runs for package.)* I have a gift. *(Unwraps paper. It is a preposterous plumed hat.)* This is such a fine hat, in this you will think fine things.

(MARY puts on hat, hugs LIZA. Exits.)

LIZA: Mary would not be mad if she thought you threw the papers in the fire to *hide* them from Father. She wouldn't be mad, Everina. We could tell her that.

EVERINA: Why not tell Mary the truth, Liza, that you sneak out to see Thomas every chance you get, and you are the one threw the papers in the fire by accident because he made you dizzy?

LIZA: I took them out again though.

(Freeze. Lights or out.)

SCENE 7

PUNCH: Mary becomes a governess in Ireland.

JUDY: Lady and Lord Kingsborough have something in common.

PUNCH: Their children! They both hate them.

JUDY: Mary tries her best to abate them.

PUNCH: *(Sourly.)* She writes "Thoughts on the Education of Daughters."

JUDY: She is bossed around and follows orders.

PUNCH: Lady Kingsborough is a witch.

JUDY: Lady Kingsborough is a bitch. *(Covers her mouth.)*

PUNCH: But there are special moments of pleasure for Mary.

JUDY: Where she is well engaged and sometimes quite merry.

SCENE 8

Lights up. MARY is in disarray, lying in the arms of GILBERT IMLAY.

LADY KINGSBOROUGH: *(Voiceover.)* Mary Wollstonecraft. You open that door this moment. I have words for you. You are not going to make me the wicked stepmother in Cinderella. Turning my daughters against me, you steal their minds. My dogs give me more love than my children. I thank God I didn't pay you to take care of my kennel!

MARY: Yes, Lady Kingsborough. I'm hurrying. *(Kisses GILBERT.)* Lady Kingsborough, I'm quite undressed. Please forgive the delay.

LADY KINGSBOROUGH: *(Voiceover.)* I won't have it, I tell you. Your ideas of womanhood! Really now. A masculine mind, Mary? A governess with a masculine mind? What is keeping you!? If you want things too much, you won't get them, miss. Mind here. If your ambitions make you hate men, you'll get nothing. Get out here.

MARY: As soon as possible, Lady Kingsborough.

(MARY and GILBERT kiss.)

LADY KINGSBOROUGH: *(Voiceover; knocking.)* If you do not open that door, it is goodbye, Mary. You write to help teachers teach children? How kind of you. You write to have parents raise their own children without servants? How good of you. We will put it into effect. Today. As soon as you leave. Get upstairs at once. *(Bangs door.)* Mary! You are needed in the drawing room to meet our houseguest Mr. Gilbert Imlay. Do you hear me, Mary?

MARY: Yes ma'am. I've already met Mr. Imlay, Lady Kingsborough, but I'll join you shortly when I am dressed properly for the important occasion. *(To GILBERT.)* How do you do, Mr. Imlay. *(Gives hand while holding bodice together.)*

GILBERT: It's been a *great* pleasure, Miss Wollstonecraft. *(Kisses her hand.)*

Anna Nicole: Blonde Glory

(excerpt)

CHARACTERS

ANNA: Thirties; big sensual blonde; wears kimono, a shift beneath for changes

PUSHKIN: Twenties to thirties; intellectual, wears sweater, collegiate

HORSHEL: Forties to fifties; Anna's manager; unkempt suit

ANIMA: Anna's dead twin; thirties; petite, dark hair, wears red wings

INTERVIEWER/DOCTOR: Male, any age; with camera in Act 1, stethoscope in Act 2

ACT 1

ANNA gets up from chaise longue. Toy box on floor.

ANNA: Hey guys, I just had the worst dream. *(Trying to recall.)* I was driving always driving and it was getting too dark and I was running out of gas and it was getting dark and on Sunday no gas stations are open at night and I had to go to the bathroom so I stopped to buy some candy. I saw a man dressed like Santa Claus, and he took off his boots, and his hat, then his belt, then all his clothes and then he said to hug him because he was Santa Claus. I didn't know what to do so I did.

PUSHKIN: You did what?

ANNA: *(Sleepily.)* I hugged him! A naked Santa. *(She shivers.)* It was awful. *(Rummages in toy box.)* I seem to have lost something. Do you know what I lost? It was right here. And everything I almost know, I forget. It could be here... *(Comes up with stuffed dog.)* OH DEAR Randy. *(Kisses dog; throws back.)*

PUSHKIN: Time for your tutorial, Anna.

HORSHEL: You're becoming a problem, Pushkin. I'll give you fifteen minutes, then you can shove your thesis up your—

ANNA: *(Interrupting.)* OH! LOOK! *(Picks up tequila bottle from toy box. Holds up, looks inside, shakes upside down.)* Why is tequila always empty? *(Throws back in box.)*

(PUSHKIN and HORSHEL move forward to talk to audience while ANNA plays with her possessions. She picks up tiara from box, looks in mirror, tries it on, throws it back. PUSHKIN and HORSHEL talk past her.)

PUSHKIN: *(To audience.)* Gentleman of the Committee: Let us say, Anna was damaged by gender. Some women are intelligent, yes. Anna... Anna is on the verge of intelligence. Thus my study.

ANNA: *(To audience.)* I think I know what's going on. Do you know what's going on?

HORSHEL: *(Disgusted.)* Anna is a financial liability. Like I tell her, Anna, you can't pray for people to love you. You can't bring out a statue of Madonna and her backup boys and kneel down to her and pray, and suddenly know how to dance.

ANNA: Hey, guys, I'm still here.

PUSHKIN: Dear Advisors, whatever moral judgments you bring here, whatever your tribunal, remember Anna's dilemma. First she had no family or real childhood—no companionship. So what possibly could be her redemption?

HORSHEL: I tell her. You got to make the stage your life. It's a chat room every minute. Chatter, chatter, chatter, Anna.

Please do something. An artist doesn't care what the world thinks. Pull your skirts up. The screen, the TV, it's all a parade of people after people after people. Who cares? But some one person watching you on TV will stop and look and say, "Now *she* is something special!" What does it mean to have everyone in the world know you? Everything! That's what!

ANNA: Can I please say something?

PUSHKIN: Human behavior that begins with fright results in splintered vision. Deprivation is on trial here, if you insist on judging Anna, at least love her. And if you ask why I cannot love her, it is because I love knowledge more: literature, philosophy, linguistics, science, and ethics, better than her— or anyone, for that matter.

ANNA: *(Looks up.)* And I really am afraid of death, you guys. Tell them that too while you're at it.

PUSHKIN: *(To audience.)* There is a black box in the lab at Princeton University made up of distorted mirrors. If you look into it, there's a photographic image. If it is someone you love, the face will not look distorted to you. Let me put it to you this way: Anna's mirror has no image whatsoever. There's a black hole always looking back at her. But, she keeps going! She is Hope itself. Bless her! Let us say, if this were the Holocaust, Anna would hang her thong on the barbed-wire fence to dry.

ANNA: I think I get it. I think I am beginning to—

HORSHEL: *(To audience.)* Frankly, as good as she looks—as big, as blonde—as dazzling as a drag queen at three a.m.—I'm told by my clients that her sex just lacks conviction. Whatever you think of her—whatever you think of me—without me she'd be just one more ice cube in Hell.

ANNA: Oh I get it. An ice cube in Hell melts...I figured that out. Right, Push? You're the professor. And HORSHEL! *(Coquettish.)* I am not going to HELL!

HORSHEL: You got five minutes with her, Pushkin. Then it's show time. *(Exiting.)*

PUSHKIN: It's always show time with you.

ANNA: I'm not going to Hell, but I'm afraid of Heaven. I'm worried about it.

PUSHKIN: Heaven? Is that what worries you? My dissertation on you is already overdue. Past due. Late. Do you hear me? Between you and your manager, I'm the one who should worry!

ANNA: I'm not just a bug under your microscope, Push. Think of this. If I'm here and if I get depressed, I got my pills, my vodka. But if something goes wrong in Heaven, I'm a goner.

PUSHKIN: Look Anna, I'm praying for you. OK?

ANNA: Why can't I ask my own self?

PUSHKIN: Oh Anna how innocent you are. I have to be the one to interpret what God says and I'll tell you what to do. Listen to me. I have advanced degrees.

ANNA: Well, what does God say?

PUSHKIN: *(Listens.)* That I, not Horshel, I should tell you what to do. That an academic knows more than a manager— *(Looks at watch.)* OMYGOD. My orals! *(Exiting.)*

ANNA: Yeah. Your orals. I hate to hurt your feelings but you're not very good at that. Maybe school can help.

HORSHEL: *(Yells from offstage.)* Anna, look alive. Press is here.

(INTERVIEWER rushes in with camera. Flashes of lights. With each question, ANNA strikes a different pose.)

INTERVIEWER: So where were you born, Anna?

ANNA: In a trailer.

INTERVIEWER: A trailer?

ANNA: Double wide.

INTERVIEWER: I mean what state.

ANNA: Texas.

INTERVIEWER: That's a big place.

ANNA: Yes. There was a school with hot trees around it.

INTERVIEWER: Where?

ANNA: There was a lot of dust in the school yard. But we moved around a lot.

INTERVIEWER: Is it true it was Beverly Hills, Texas?

ANNA: I call it that, yeah.

INTERVIEWER: Any street signs you can remember? This is for the *Global Inquiry*. Think, Anna. People want to picture you at home.

ANNA: *(Trying.)* There was... um... an old car in the yard, and... um... a refrig on the porch, and... um... OH! There was this big old colored rainbow that came out after it rained. It was so beautiful all glowing. That's where I lived. I loved the colors in the mist so much.

INTERVIEWER: Well thanks, that pins it down. What did you want, say, when you were five years old?

ANNA: I think I just wanted to make it to six. I got beaten up so much. I got on my parents' nerves.

INTERVIEWER: There's a rumor you lost a child once. Any truth to that?

ANNA: *(Flares.)* That is a dirty rotten filthy lie. I got one son a beautiful grown manchild. He's coming to visit me any day now.

INTERVIEWER: So what do you want now, Anna?

ANNA: Oh I want to be happy, very very happy, and then I'll fit my career in around that.

INTERVIEWER: *(Exiting.)* You know what? I hope you get it, Anna. You're a sweet kid. A really sweet kid.

ANNA: *(Touched.)* I think he liked me. *(Calling.)* HORSHEL! He liked me. I think.

(In jumps ANIMA.)

ANIMA: I hate it when you start lying in public.

ANNA: Then where should I do it? *(Confused.)* Wait! I was not lying. Our parents beat the shit out of me every day and you know it.

ANIMA: Angels don't like dirty laundry.

ANNA: HOW did you get in my room again? Leave me alone, PLEASE. Hors! Pushkin! Help.

ANIMA: They can't see me honey, so go embarrass yourself— go ahead, make my eternity.

ANNA: You seem to forget. You're dead.

ANIMA: Right.

ANNA: You died at birth. You DIED at birth!

ANIMA: Yup. Our mother will never forgive you for being the one left.

ANNA: My identical twin. *(Shudders.)* I can't believe it.

ANIMA: *(Dryly.)* As close as they could get.

ANNA: Why can't you stay dead? Just this once please. I'm on my way to something big. I want this job so much, Horshel has an audition set for me.

ANIMA: Now what exactly is it that you want so fucking bad?

ANNA: I have a dream.

ANIMA: A dream? A dream!! She has a dream!

ANNA: Why not? *(Flash of anger.)* Even birds have dreams.

ANIMA: About worms. Birds dream about worms.

ANNA: Maybe that's true, but it's their dreams and they have a right. Listen, I'm going to audition for the Hippodrome and if you could just this once not get in my way, nothing personal against you—but I need this chance to show my stuff, to show that I can sing and dance. That I'm more than a PETA spokesperson.

ANIMA: Sure. I think I can help.

ANNA: NO. No thanks! No help. Just like go someplace. A vacation for a while.

ANIMA: No can do. But I can stay and help.

ANNA: Anima, I'm begging you this time. I'm scared. I am really really scared.

ANIMA: OK. First. Here's a little pill. *(Hands pill bottle.)* Take it.

ANNA: Another little pill? That's what you've been giving me and after a while I always wind up in a room as big as a cell.

ANIMA: Oh, before, that was just so you'd have fun, for recreation. This is to give you confidence.

ANNA: Confidence.

ANIMA: You know the stuff other people have, mostly important men. Where they can say and do anything and not feel ashamed, even after they're exposed on TV for whatever they did wrong.

ANNA: *(Thoughtful.)* Not feel ashamed?

ANIMA: Would be great, yes? *(Pours pills into ANNA's hand.)*

ANNA: But Anima, I don't get it. *(Looks at hand.)* If I'm scared before I take the pills, and then after I take the pills, I'm not scared...then who am I? Which person?

ANIMA: *(Sweetly.)* The one who doesn't feel shame after.

ANNA: OK I'll try. *(Swallows handful. Flops down.)*

ANIMA: And for the sake of decency, when you sit down, keep your skirt between your legs. Angels don't like crotches.

ANNA: You know, that interviewer liked me. I know he did. And I was so happy and just when everything goes so good, then you— *(Looks at pills.)* and so what do you want from me? For these? People keep giving me stuff I don't want to get something from me I don't want to give. This keeps happening to me.

ANIMA: *(Exits.)* Angels don't like complaints.

ANNA: *(Jumps up and runs after.)* Wait wait ANIMA! COME BACK. How many pills do I take to not feel shame? HELP. What do I do with these? WHEN? COME BACK HELP! *(She goes to each corner calling her back.)* COME HERE THIS MINUTE. You can't leave me like this.

(Enter HORSHEL.)

HORSHEL: What the hell is all this screaming about? *(Accusingly.)* Drugs?!

ANNA: No thanks Horshel. I have some.

HORSHEL: Get up and look alive. I have it!

ANNA: You have what?

HORSHEL: Pop Porn! I may have a backer. The product. For YOU. To put your name in every TV room. Something people can eat while they watch you on TV. POP PORN! They put it in the microwave while they watch you having sex on video.

ANNA: Buttered? That's fattening. You wanted me to lose weight. It's not even real butter and the salt isn't even...

HORSHEL: Anna, this is what we need. A product we can sell besides your body. Something people can chew on besides your body. Something with a fragrance.

ANNA: Besides my body. I don't know...

HORSHEL: Imagine it on every shelf in the video store.

ANNA: *(Excitedly.)* Blockbusters?

HORSHEL: Um... No not that one. Some other ones. I am wild with the idea. I have to call the graphics people.

ANNA: Do we kitchen test it? And I talk about it then? On TV? In an apron?

HORSHEL: Not your worry, my little flower. We just need your photo on the bag.

ANNA: I have a beautiful idea for a picture.

HORSHEL: Breasts. A picture of your breasts.

ANNA: I was thinking of boats. I like happy boats.

HORSHEL: No Anna.

ANNA: Sailors would like it.

HORSHEL: Breasts.

ANNA: With happy boats in the background and maybe a sun?

HORSHEL: Just the breasts, Anna, POP PORN. You will be famous yet!

ANNA: I'm not too sure about the picture on the bag.

HORSHEL: Breasts, Anna, which one of us knows more, lived near a college? Me or you?

Pinecrest Rest Haven

Thornton Wilder said "Love has no need for memory." In Pinecrest Rest Haven, Mr. and Mrs. P no longer remember they're married, and they fall in love (and hate) again and again. Residents have all the greed, betrayal, and lust they ever had when young.

CHARACTERS

MR. P: Elderly character

MRS. P: Elderly character

YOUNG MR. P: Thirty years old, 1940s garb

YOUNG MRS. P: Twenty to thirty years old, 1940s clothing

COCO: Elderly woman

MURIEL: Elderly woman

KRISTAL: Young nurse

DOCTOR: Young woman

CHUCK: Elderly man

ACT 1

SCENE: Pinecrest Rest Haven sunroom. MRS. P is center stage.

MRS. P: I'm here looking for Mr. P. Have you seen him? He's about this high and goes all the way to the floor. He left home one day to go to the store. Of course he went every day where the pretty girl sold fish. He would buy one oyster each day and when I complained, he changed to shrimp. Then he didn't come back at all. They invited me in to stay here. I need to find him, to take him home.

(Enter MR. P opposite side of stage.)

MR. P: She was the cutest thing you'd ever see, hair like a halo, or a sunrise. To be next to her was to be the right tempera-ture, like your blood was the same as the air outside. A perfect day is what she was. A perfect day.

MRS. P: Once I said, aren't you ever going to kiss me, and he put his hand under my chin and lifted it up just a little and placed his face near mine. We were on a small bridge over some water. The water moved on and on and brought me here. Love was like a slipcover all over me then.

SCENE: Sunroom dark. In front of scrim is a park bench. YOUNG MR. P is hiding behind tree. YOUNG MRS. P walks nervously on, looks about, sits on bench. YOUNG MR. P saun-ters out casually, wearing WWII uniform.

YOUNG MR. P: Oh hello there.

(YOUNG MRS. P looks away. YOUNG MR. P sits beside her. She gets up.)

YOUNG MRS. P: I don't believe we've met.

(Curtain up. Bench becomes part of dayroom décor with pillow added. YOUNG MR. P and YOUNG MRS. P go to either side of stage. All characters are onstage milling about. COCO and MURIEL walk through center, MURIEL carrying a stuffed dog.)

COCO: Did Room 7b die or was he faking again?

MURIEL: He did. Even rich people die.

COCO: But he was cheap. He only died because it's free.

MURIEL: You're just mad because dead people don't listen to you anymore.

COCO: Stop kissing that damn animal. Do you know where its mouth has been!?

MURIEL: I'll put him down then.

COCO: Not there, for god's sake. Someone messed on the seat.

(MR. P and MRS. P cross from opposite sides of stage, pass each other, stop, look back at each other quizzically. Turn back and continue walking. They stop briefly.)

MR. P: Hello.

MRS. P: Hello.

MR. P: How are you.

MRS. P: How are you.

(YOUNG MR. P and YOUNG MRS. P trail them like angels, mime greeting with identical moves, as MR. P and MRS. P go to either side of stage or off.)

COCO: They said he had a fit and died right here, screaming and moaning and holding his sides, foaming at the mouth.

MURIEL: *(Blasé.)* I hate that.

(Characters clear center where focus is on KRISTAL and DOCTOR. COCO and MURIEL drift off. MR. P and MRS. P take chairs at opposite sides.)

DOCTOR: *(Hands KRISTAL file folder.)* We must discharge a patient.

KRISTAL: What do you mean, discharge a patient?

DOCTOR: We have too much dead meat and not enough beds.

KRISTAL: Well we can scarcely—

DOCTOR: I am the doctor and I'll make the diagnosis.

KRISTAL: Who did you have in mind? Not Mr. P over there?

(MR. P is settled in his chair, falling asleep.)

DOCTOR: Oh heavens no, he'd never find his way to the lobby.

KRISTAL: *(Indicating MRS. P.)* Not Mrs. P? He'd die without her.

(They walk off, KRISTAL following DOCTOR.)

DOCTOR: Not enough beds, too many bodies.

(COCO and MURIEL drift off. MR. P and MRS. P are seated on opposite sides of the room. YOUNG MR. P and YOUNG MRS. P are seated behind them. MR. P crosses to MRS. P; MRS. P crosses to meet MR. P in center.)

MR. P: Are you new here?

MRS. P: I think so.

MR. P: What're you in for?

MRS. P: I think I'm trying to improve myself.

MR. P: Do you feel things sometimes?

MRS. P: Oh yes. I feel so many things, they have to take turns.

MR. P: What are they?

MRS. P: Oh I can't remember.

MR. P: *(Delighted.)* Me either!

MRS. P: I have a picture of two people. *(Brings it to him.)*

MR. P: In a husband and wife costume! She's pretty.

MRS. P: I think it used to be me.

MR. P: Nice man with her.

MRS. P: I'm not real sure, but I think that used to be you.

MR. P: We can ask the postman about that card.

MRS. P: I wish there'd be stewed tomatoes for supper, don't you? I used to know how to make them. My mother taught me when we lived in Vermont, on a yellow tablecloth. You went to the country and turned left. That's where Vermont is.

MR. P: *(Still puzzling over wedding picture.)* I have a postcard just like that in my room.

MRS. P: We must have been to the same place.

MR. P: Once.

MRS. P: But that was then.

MR. P: Will you be my beloved wife?

MRS. P: *(Demure.)* I don't talk to strangers.

(CHUCK wanders through.)

CHUCK: Where did everyone go? Where is everyone? Where does everyone always go... *(Wanders off.)*

MRS. P: *(To CHUCK.)* Oh please don't feel anything. It'll just make it worse.

SCENE: MR. P is snoozing in his chair by the window. MRS. P is on the other side of the room, knitting confusedly. COCO reenters center door, followed by MURIEL.

COCO: Do you see him?

MURIEL: Who?

COCO: The only him here.

MURIEL: Oh him.

COCO: Look how innocent he's acting.

MURIEL: He's asleep.

COCO: That's what he'd like you to believe.

MURIEL: He's snoring. *(Powdering her nose, looking in her mirror.)*

COCO: You don't need to try to get his attention.

MURIEL: I don't need you to tell me what to do.

COCO: This is how he fools everyone.

MURIEL: Why does he want to, Coco?

COCO: Because, Muriel, he's stalking me. No matter what room I'm in, there he is. I'm about to report him.

MURIEL: For sleeping?

COCO: For stalking, stupid. Everyone has his individual style. He is especially crafty at it, as you can see.

MURIEL: And what of her? *(Indicating MRS. P.)*

COCO: Mrs. P? Ha. He doesn't even remember he's married to her. Besides, she's not worth stalking. She's easy with him, I hear.

MURIEL: We have only three rooms we can be in this time of day, sunroom, dining room, craft room. So Mr. P is bound to be in one of them.

COCO: Ha! He's drawn you in too, has he? Isn't he clever now?

(COCO walks over and sprays perfume on herself, close to him. MR. P coughs from it, shifts, returns to sleep.)

COCO: See? Quite the pretender, isn't he.

(COCO storms out with MURIEL following. MRS. P moves across the room, coughs. MR. P opens his eyes.)

MRS. P: Hello.

MRS. P: How are you?

MR. P: Never better. Never better.

MRS. P: Everyone wants my boyfriend but Mr. P just wants me. (To him.) Don't you. When we leave here we're going to every Shoney's in the USA. Every one. And we'll leave a tip.

SCENE: Circle.

CHUCK: I raised my children. I went to a job every day for forty-three years.

COCO: I once was an editor for a newsletter. It went to six hundred people.

MRS. P: Everything I say he says the opposite. I say the sun glimpsed in the window. He says no. It peeked.

COCO: Peeked is my word (Turns to MURIEL.) Didn't you hear me say it before, Muriel? Peeked is my word.

MURIEL: (To MR. P.) My friend likes you.

CHUCK: I sent money home every week to my wife without fail.

MURIEL: I had a white satin coat I wore on Times Square at midnight New Year's Eve.

COCO: I had a red roadster. The top came down.

CHUCK: Once I rode across the country on boxcars to find a job. I was younger then.

COCO: I had three cats in one window.

MRS. P: I had a green plant in my window.

MR. P: It was on the counter.

MRS. P: See? Always contrary.

CHUCK: I saw a boat once filled with snow in Wisconsin.

MURIEL: *(Fading.)* I had...

MRS. P: It was in the window.

MR. P: I'm afraid to die.

MRS. P: I'm afraid I won't die. We'll just go on here forever.

DOCTOR: Why are you sad. You have everything you want here.

CHUCK: I have dreams of galloping horses.

DOCTOR: Just eat and sleep whenever you want.

MR. P: I WANT TO DIFFER.

DOCTOR: Nothing human is wrong.

MRS. P: If he drops the paper I pick it up. He pushes me away and says he doesn't need help. If he drops the paper and I don't pick it up, he says why doesn't anyone ever help me.

DOCTOR: We're going to have to move you to a different sunroom.

MRS. P: Something's gone wrong with us, but I can't leave.

DOCTOR: It's time to try something new.

(Scene freezes, or group leaves. MR. P remains at one side of room. MRS. P at other. Half light. YOUNG MR. P enters in WWII uniform. YOUNG MRS. P enters. They move to center bench. She sits first. He joins her.)

YOUNG MR. P: Hello.

YOUNG MRS. P: Hello.

YOUNG MR. P: You were here yesterday.

YOUNG MRS. P: I'm waiting for someone. He said five p.m. I wonder if I have the wrong day.

YOUNG MR. P: Candy bar?

YOUNG MRS. P: Why thank you, I'll share.

YOUNG MR. P: No need. *(Shows a second bar.)*

(They eat in silence.)

YOUNG MR. P: I'm not taking the bus.

YOUNG MRS. P: You're not?

YOUNG MR. P: I passed here twice this week and saw you sitting. I'm not here for a bus.

YOUNG MRS. P: And you said here's a chippie. Well you can just move on and fast talk someone else. *(Gets up.)*

YOUNG MR. P: No, I swear—

YOUNG MRS. P: I'm calling the law.

YOUNG MR. P: *(Laughing.)* I like a high-tempered gal. But I'm innocent except for thinking—she's a beauty. I'll move on now.

(Young Mrs. P walks away.)

YOUNG MR. P: I saw no one came for you.

YOUNG MRS. P: That is not your business. Who does or does not get off the bus or who I'm waiting for or not waiting for.

YOUNG MR. P: He's not coming. Not today. Or not tomorrow.

YOUNG MRS. P: *(Exiting.)* Police.

YOUNG MR. P: *(Calling after.)* I meant no harm. I saw you. I know you work at Woolworth's. I didn't want to get your goat, honest... *(Fading.)* I thought, "She's a real looker, that one."

YOUNG MRS. P: *(Offstage.)* Fresh!

(Lights fade; music: "I'm in Love with You, Honey."

SCENE: Sunroom. MRS. P moves closer.

MRS. P: Do you happen to have the time.

MR. P: *(Looks at watch.)* It's 1932.

MRS. P: That was nice then.

MR. P: Yes, sun on the streets then. Leaves in the fall stacked up on the sidewalk.

MRS. P: That was pretty yes. There was a house with a yellow tablecloth inside.

MR. P: I'm onto you. You get me to agree and then you start crying. No. Not today, old lady. You won't get me that way— oh no, not today.

MRS. P: I was only remembering.

MR. P: No such thing, remembering. You get there or you get here. Two places to be. One makes you cry.

MRS. P: What time is it then. What time could it be.

MR. P: It's the same time it always was. Hungry time, sad time. It's the same time it always was, sleeptime, no time, less time, more time, lost time, new time.

MRS. P: You never hold a proper conversation with me anymore. You fill me with sorrow.

MR. P: Sorrow. That's the color of your damn tablecloth, and you can't trick me into talking about it either.

(KRISTAL bounces in center door with huge beach ball.)

KRISTAL: Kristal here. Healthy minds, healthy bodies.

(She bounces ball to MR. P. He lets it drop without attempting to get it. Ball bounces to MRS. P. She covers her face in protection and lets it hit her.)

KRISTAL: Better! Better! You're getting it. Now we're going to go to step two.

(KRISTAL pulls chair over. Seats MRS. P opposite MR. P.)

KRISTAL: I'm going to give you the letter and you give me the state. "M." *(Bounces ball to MRS. P.)* Maine. See how it'll go? Now your turn *(Bounces ball to MRS. P again.)* "P."

MRS. P: *(Flustered.)* Potato. Portland. Pie.

(COCO and MURIEL entering, start giggling. MRS. P spins around.)

MRS. P: They confused me.

LOUDSPEAKER: *(Voiceover.)* Love Alert. Love Alert. Kristal needed in cafeteria, egg fight Table 17. Kristal.

(KRISTAL runs out. MURIEL and COCO circle MRS. P menacingly.)

COCO: I see you have your padded bra on today, Mrs. P. Don't you look fine. You must be expecting a big day.

MURIEL: All dressed up. Going somewhere? Your grand-daughter visiting?

COCO: I think it's her great-great-great-granddaughter by now, if in fact there's one at all.

MRS. P: What do you want?

COCO: I have a little bone to pick with you.

MRS. P: Out of my way, you...you fireplug.

MURIEL: *(Blocks door.)* This is the only way out.

COCO: *(Holds up pocketbook.)* What is this? A pocketbook? Yes?

MRS. P: Everybody knows what that is.

COCO: You stole my word for it. I call it a purse and now I hear YOU calling it a purse.

MURIEL: That's plagiary. I know because I used to live in New York. My husband owned the Barbizon Plaza.

COCO: Shut up, you idiot.

MURIEL: Well he did.

COCO: We don't need your résumé.

MRS. P: If you don't get out of my way, I'll use my purse where it'll do the most good. *(Raises it to hit her.)*

(Not knowing what to do, MR. P has been removing his clothes in the background. He stands and dramatically drops his pants. All scream but MRS. P, who goes over to him. The rest scramble.)

MRS. P: *(Whispers.)* You always were my hero. You'll get chilly *(She pulls his pants up to his waist.)*

COCO: *(To MURIEL.)* See? He's always trying to show me "something."

MURIEL: I had a good husband once in New York City. Manhattan it was called then.

COCO: *(To MRS. P.)* I'm not finished with you. *(Holds up purse.)* PURSE. That's my word. Yours was POCKETBOOK. I distinctly heard you say that out loud. Then all of a sudden you started calling it a *purse*. I've reported you and you probably will be put out on the street.

(MRS. P rips COCO's purse from her, opens it, and dumps the contents on the floor. MRS. P smells the empty purse inside.)

MRS. P: Smells like adultery in there. Stay away from Mr. P, while you're at it. *(Drops purse over side of stage.)* There are some things worse to lose than your life, you know. For instance, your PURSE.

(She sails out, then looks back as if she's forgotten something. Goes back to MR. P. He's still holding onto his pants. She puts her arm in his free arm and begins to walk him out with great dignity. MURIEL is putting on lipstick. COCO takes pencil out from behind her ear, puts it in her mouth like a cigarette, striking a pose, as if she doesn't care. She then runs to look for purse.)

COCO: *(Hisses after MRS. P.)* Potato isn't a state, stupid.

(MRS. P turns back to confront COCO—glares. COCO begins to arrange flowers in the vase innocently.)

SCENE: DOCTOR and KRISTAL carry on chairs, center, forming a semicircle facing the audience.

DOCTOR AND KRISTAL: *(Call out each door.)* Group time.

(MRS. P puts lipstick on, straightens skirt.)

LOUDSPEAKER: *(Voiceover.)* Come alive Section Five. It's your group therapy meeting time.

(MR. P has to be pulled physically against his will to the group. He is muttering that he has an important conference call. COCO and MURIEL sashay to seats on either side of MR. P. Light on MRS. P.)

MRS. P: I don't know why I'm here. I know there is something I miss. Someone I used to know who's gone. I think it's me. *(Weeping.)*

KRISTAL: We have some new members joining us today.

MR. P: We don't want any.

KRISTAL: Let's all tell one thing about ourselves. This is Chuck.

(CHUCK is slouched down in chair with hat and dark glasses.)

KRISTAL: Chuck was in the entertainment business.

CHUCK: I was the lead guitarist in Kate Smith's band.

KRISTAL: That's good. That's good.

CHUCK: Well, actually I was his cousin.

KRISTAL: That's close. Close is good. And what do you feel about being here.

CHUCK: Hungry.

KRISTAL: That's not an emotion, Chuck.

COCO: I knew you were famous.

CHUCK: I have to wear these sunglasses at all times.

COCO: You had a roast named after you, didn't you? I used to buy it at FoodLand.

MURIEL: I've heard of that. Chuck roast. Yes, named after him?

(Group gets excited. Starts chanting "Chuck, Chuck, Chuck.")

KRISTAL: Let's get back to our feelings about being here.

MR. P: Shitty.

MRS. P: Tired.

COCO: Chuck Chuck Chuck *(Stands up, pointing.)*

(Others start standing and chanting: "Chuck Chuck Chuck," approaching him. CHUCK pulls his hat down in front of his eyes, then stands. By this time, the group is all standing and pointing at him.)

KRISTAL: Let's all be seated. *(Shouting above the din.)* Or I'll have to bring out the games.

MR. P: No. No crafts. Please. We'll be quiet. *(Thinks of ploy; stands.)* I used to be an important man. I had a secretary, a dictaphone, a nameplate on my desk, a secretary who didn't wear underpants but that's another story. Once I was nominated the most important man in the Chamber of Commerce.

MRS. P: He nominated himself.

MR. P: But I was nominated. That's the important thing.

MRS. P: Somebody is trying to confuse us.

COCO: I'm only here temporarily. The cruise line was booked.

MURIEL: That's not why you're here.

(Noise subsides.)

KRISTAL: Now then. Chuck. How do you feel about being here?

(Silence. CHUCK has his face in his hands.)

ALL: Oh. He likes it. *(Murmurs of agreement and approval.)*

KRISTAL: But he's crying. Does that mean he likes it? Are we sure that's what we're feeling?

(All register looks of confusion.)

KRISTAL: *(Changes mood.)* Well now, what is today? Anyone.

COCO: Now.

MRS. P: *(Stands.)* That's not fair. She remembered that answer from before.

COCO: It's always now.

KRISTAL: That's right. Any questions?

(Freeze scene. Lights down.)

SCENE: MRS. P walks to another space where the DOCTOR is seated at her desk.)

MRS. P: I wanted to talk to you.

DOCTOR: Yes yes indeed.

MRS. P: I wanted to talk to you about—

DOCTOR: Yes?

MRS. P: About the past. No one will talk to me about *(Voice breaking.)* the past.

DOCTOR: The past.

MRS. P: Yes.

DOCTOR: The past does not exist.

MRS. P: But I remember things.

DOCTOR: There is only now.

MRS. P: Well, can we talk about the now that used to be?

(DOCTOR shakes head no.)

MRS. P: About the now that's going to be?

DOCTOR: No. If you will not be quiet about this, you'll go to the opportunity room. Do you need to go...

MRS. P: No.

DOCTOR: Let us start again. It is always the present. Time is now. It doesn't matter what happened before you got here. We're one big happy family right now.

MRS. P: You mean this is all there is?

DOCTOR: This is all there is. Now.

MRS. P: There was more before I got to this place. *(Subdued.)* I'm afraid of the now that is. Nurse, be nice. Let me talk to the doctor.

DOCTOR: I am the doctor.

MRS. P: But you're a girl. There must be someone in charge.

DOCTOR: Mrs. P, don't you want to keep learning? Don't you want to grow?

MRS. P: Oh I got you there, nursie, you don't grow anymore after you reach sixty. I'm as tall as I'm going to get.

(Bell rings.)

LOUDSPEAKER: *(Voiceover; sing-song voice.)* Today we're having tryouts for a play. Don't be afraid. Don't think about the past. Don't be afraid to fail. Pick a person you'd like to be and come to the costume room in the back of the craft gallery and go through the trunk and see who you'd like to be.

SCENE: *Marriage ceremony of YOUNG MR. P and YOUNG MRS. P. He's in uniform; she's in pleated skirt, jacket, hat and corsage.*

MINISTER: *(Voiceover.)* Till death us do part.

YOUNG MRS. P: That's a very long time.

YOUNG MR. P: Now's no time to argue, darling.

MINISTER: *(Voiceover.)* Do you or don't you.

YOUNG MRS. P: I do.

YOUNG MR. P: I do.

SCENE: *Table and chairs. MR. P's jacket hung over chair. He sits, shirt unbuttoned, head in his arms. On table, a bottle.*

YOUNG MRS. P: It's a two-day pass and you've slept it away.

(She takes his jacket, tidies up. Photo falls out. She looks, tears it up, pours it over him like confetti. She puts on her jacket to leave. He shakes himself awake, realizes, sees pieces, laughing.)

YOUNG MR. P: No NO. This is my sister Camille, my only sister. *(Pulls YOUNG MRS. P on his lap.)* Poor little chickie. You're always so scared the bus won't come or always afraid I've made someone else happy. *(Takes her arm.)* C'mon. Let's dance.

YOUNG MRS. P: Not this time.

YOUNG MR. P: It's the dance we do. Nobody's here but me and you.

YOUNG MRS. P: How do you think I can forget things in a moment?

YOUNG MR. P: But now is now. Whatever happened yesterday is gone. This is all we have.

YOUNG MRS. P: When I'm hurt I'm hurt. I can't forget this quick.

YOUNG MR. P: Yes you can. Try.

(He takes her, swirls her; she reluctantly joins in the dance.)

SCENE: COCO and MURIEL are rummaging through the trunk. COCO brings out a Spanish shawl.

COCO: What are you going to be in the play?

MURIEL: Myself.

COCO: You're supposed to play a part.

MURIEL: What part am I not playing?

COCO: You have to pretend you're someone else.

MURIEL: I'm not who you think, Coco. I used to be wealthy.

COCO: I know. Filthy rich. Emphasis on filthy.

MURIEL: What a naughty thing to say.

COCO: Who am I? *(Picks a stuffed doll from trunk, boo hoos into it.)*

MURIEL: Raggedy Ann's mother?

COCO: No, silly. You know who I am, acting like this? *(Cradles and rocks the doll.)*

(MRS. P appears at door.)

MRS. P: My baby is all grown up now, thank you, and she's coming to visit, soon.

COCO AND MURIEL: *(Snicker.)* Yes yes. Like the last time you sat by the door all Sunday.

MRS. P: She has a big job across the country but now she's coming and she'll take me out for breakfast or lunch or dinner or a walk and a talk.

COCO: *(Sings.)* I'll believe it when I see it.

MRS. P: She'll be here soon.

(COCO and MURIEL exit. KRISTAL walks through.)

MRS. P: Excuse me.

KRISTAL: Yes.

MRS. P: We're going to put on a play.

KRISTAL: Wonderful. But I'm in a hurry now. Pill time.

MRS. P: I need you to be in it.

KRISTAL: I don't really have the time.

MRS. P: I need you to be in my play.

KRISTAL: You're serious, Mrs. P.

MRS. P: *(Grabs her arm.)* Please. I'll pay you. I'll give you my dessert. I'll save it off the table. A new fresh sweet dessert.

KRISTAL: *(Touched.)* What part did you want me to play?

MRS. P: I need you to be my daughter.

SCENE: MRS. P alone on stage.

MRS. P: Today I pretended to get up, eat breakfast. That was the truth. Sewed a quilt, made cranberry jelly, saw an angel in the window, wrote a letter. This is not true. Took a nap, that part is true too, fed the cats, covered the couch with the quilt, let the cat sit there on the couch, ate the cranberry jelly, went for a walk, no I didn't, saw a neighbor, talked to her, told her who I am, who I used to be. She said she used to know me. You see? I am a person. I think this is true.

(DOCTOR enters. Seats MRS. P.)

DOCTOR: What season is this?

MRS. P: There's snow outside so I'm sure it's winter. If it were summer, you see, the sun would—

DOCTOR: Yes. Yes. Who is president of the United States?

MRS. P: *(Silence.)* Now?

DOCTOR: Now. *(Writes.)*

(Silence.)

DOCTOR: People basically good or bad?

MRS. P: Good. I'm sure they are. When I was small there was...

DOCTOR: Yes, yes. Now, are people mostly happy or sad?

MRS. P: I'm afraid they're sad. No? That was the wrong answer? Well of course some days they could be happy.

DOCTOR: Is it better to be young or old?

MRS. P: Oh young, I remember that answer.

DOCTOR: You may go now.

MRS. P: Did I pass the test today?

DOCTOR: I'm afraid not.

MRS. P: Not again?

DOCTOR: I'm afraid not.

(MRS. P runs from the room. KRISTAL enters.)

KRISTAL: What has her so upset?

DOCTOR: She thinks people are good and she does not acknowledge her well-being. This lady cannot be released from her old ward.

KRISTAL: But that's how it seems to her.

DOCTOR: We don't feed fantasies here, Kristal. We get people into reality. We don't crawl in their dementia with them. Some of us have to remain outside.

(KRISTAL tries to storm out. CHUCK stops KRISTAL.)

CHUCK: Excuse me.

KRISTAL: Yes Chuck?

CHUCK: Sit down, sit down.

KRISTAL: I'm on my rounds, Chuck. I just have a minute.

CHUCK: I like your dress.

KRISTAL: It's just a uniform.

CHUCK: But it's pretty. I like white, all shades of white.

KRISTAL: Thank you.

CHUCK: Especially over the top.

KRISTAL: *(Self-consciously.)* Is there something you wanted to discuss?

CHUCK: Well I thought there might be something you wanted to say. This is your chance.

KRISTAL: I think I will have to continue this later.

CHUCK: Don't go. I've noticed how you look at me. I realize this is a delicate situation. That's why I pulled you over here near the garbage where it's quiet.

KRISTAL: Chuck, I don't think—

CHUCK: Don't deny it. Your eyes follow my every move. You know even famous people need love. What I'm proposing is that you try not to think of me as anyone special. Just a guy offering his heart to a girl. Two lonely people in the midst of a crowd.

KRISTAL: A heart is a special gift. I don't take it lightly, Chuck.

CHUCK: You know I'm not all that old.

KRISTAL: Of course you're not.

CHUCK: I still wake up with an erection.

KRISTAL: Good for you.

CHUCK: Well a partial one.

KRISTAL: That's still good. Partial's good.

CHUCK: I like to be perfectly honest.

KRISTAL: A fine quality in a man.

CHUCK: Do you think we could go out sometime? If you want to, that is. I'm not all that old. I'm only here because I'm not what I used to be.

KRISTAL: Well, no one is, Chuck.

CHUCK: No one is what I used to be?

KRISTAL: I'm really honored, honestly I am, but rules are rules. We are not allowed to fraternize with the residents.

CHUCK: We don't have to fraternize. Just go out.

KRISTAL: We'll see. I have to be going.

CHUCK: I'm going to leave this place soon and I'm going to take you with me.

KRISTAL: OK. 'Bye. We'll talk later.

CHUCK: *(Calls after her.)* I like your dress. The top. I never thought I'd be the man I am. I'm not who you think I am. I'm better. I'm younger than I look. I'll get out of here. You'll see. I'm leaving this place one way or another. With or without you. I'm not staying here. I'm not wasting a partial erection. *(Exits.)*

SCENE: Sunroom. MR. P is fiddling with a flower, examining it petal by petal. MRS. P picks a flower out of the vase to sing into it like a mic. She dances around MR. P to get his attention. She peeks over her shoulder at him coquettishly and sings.

MRS. P: I'm in love with you, honey
Say you love me too, honey?
No one else will do, honey
It's funny but it's true
Loved you from the start, honey
Bless your little heart, honey

(He joins her.)

MRS. P AND MR. P: Everyday will be so sunny, honey, with you.

MRS. P: You know that song?

MR. P: All three verses.

MRS. P: It's a miracle. To meet someone in this day and age who knows the same song.

MR. P: You know what?

MRS. P: What old man?

MR. P: You know what?

MRS. P: What?

MR. P: I really really miss Bing Crosby.

MRS. P: I know. I know.

MR. P: But—

MRS. P: Yes?

MR. P: I can't think of the name for things *(Holds up flower.)* like this microphone.

MRS. P: *(Beaming.)* It's a flower.

MR. P: *(Happy then.)* What kind?

MRS. P: Yellow.

MR. P: *(Delighted.)* We make a good team, you and me. Together we can find out the names of things we lost. *(Unbuttons shirt.)* Look. *(Points at chest.)* I'm a person. See? I'm still a man, aren't I?

(YOUNG MR. P and YOUNG MRS. P are behind them in pantomime.)

MRS. P: Oh yes, and a very handsome one at that. *(Goes behind his chair and brings out plastic bag and dumps content at his feet.)* I brought everything out of my top drawer to show you. *(Holds up photo.)*

MR. P: I have that same picture!

MRS. P: I know. I know.

(She hands him items; he fondles them with confusion. KRISTAL comes in with unplugged telephone.)

KRISTAL: Here's the phone you ordered, Mr. P. For your business deals. *(Exits.)*

(MR. P looks around for a plug and finally decides on the vase of flowers.)

MRS. P: Why do you need a phone? We don't know anyone anymore.

(Sly YOUNG MR. P whispers an answer into MR. P's ear.)

MR. P: I used to have a business and still have things to do. I have to call a temp.

(Angry YOUNG MRS. P whispers into MRS. P's ear.)

MRS. P: A temp?

MR. P: A secretary temp, not one you have to keep around and feed or anything. A teenager...blonde...green eyes, if they still have them.

(Angry YOUNG MRS. P whispers into MRS. P's ear. MRS. P stuffs belongings back in bag and storms away.)

MR. P: *(Looks at phone.)* Why do they tear the numbers off? I'll put my own on. *(Looks in pocket for pen. Scribbles on center of phone.)*

MRS. P: *(Calls back.)* Teenagers do not have pictures of you in their top drawers. Teenagers do not know all the words to "I'm in Love with You, Honey."

(CHUCK comes in, trying to be incognito, sits. MRS. P rushes to him, flashing haughty look at MR. P. Pulls chair over to CHUCK.)

MRS. P: Do you phone temporary secretaries?

(CHUCK is perplexed.)

MRS. P: Good. Can I sit? *(Pulls chair closer.)* Would you like me to be interesting? *(She thinks of how.)*

(CHUCK is perplexed.)

MRS. P: *(Rummaging in handbag.)* Let's see. Would you like to look at the picture? Here are some old postcards. This one says "See Lookout Mountain Tennessee." Why do you think they want us to see that?

(CHUCK is confused. Shakes head.)

MRS. P: And this. Do you like this? It has a picture. Don't mess with Texas. See? There's the state. Don't mess with Texas. How could I do that? A big state like that. A little person like me?

(MR. P comes over with phone, quizzically. YOUNG MR. P whispers into his ear as if feeding him an idea.)

MR. P: *(To MRS. P; roars.)* Remember me?

(MRS. P freezes him out. She Turns to CHUCK, who has fallen asleep or has pulled down his hat.)

MRS. P: Excuse the interruption. He is so rude.

MR. P: *(Sings.)* I'm in love with you, honey...

(YOUNG MRS. P whispers into MRS. P's ear, feeding her an idea.)

MRS. P: *(To MR. P.)* I don't know what you're talking about. Call up your friend and sing it to her. *(Exits.)*

MR. P: *(To telephone.)* Hello? Is anyone out there?

CHUCK: Is anyone out there?

(Enter from center YOUNG MR. P and YOUNG MRS. P. Each goes to their older counterpart. KRISTAL walks through. MR. P is blowing a kiss to someone, mouthing "I love you" to KRISTAL.)

YOUNG MRS. P: You are not trustworthy.

YOUNG MR. P: I am so. This is what trustworthy looks like.

YOUNG MRS. P: I heard you tell the nurse you loved her.

YOUNG MR. P: If you weren't eavesdropping, you wouldn't have heard anything wrong.

YOUNG MRS. P: You put your hand in the cookie jar and I caught you. I saw you.

YOUNG MR. P: If you weren't watching you wouldn't see it, so it wouldn't have happened.

(YOUNG MR. P delivers a box to MR. P.)

MR. P: *(Picks up box, dumps it out.)* Mrs., you see this box. I'm going to fill it with a song you like and put it under your grave when you die so when anyone steps on it, it'll play "I'm in Love with You, Honey." *(He gets up to dance with the box.)*

MRS. P: *(Leaving.)* I'd rather you be faithful when I'm alive.

MR. P: That is not future thinking. And stop chasing me across the room.

MRS. P: I'd leave you in a minute but I have no place else to go.

MR. P: Then go there anyway. I have places I can go. (Indicates different chairs.) Here or there...

(She moves to exit. YOUNG MR. P eggs him on, gesturing "Go on. Go on. Go after her.")

MR. P: Girlie. Don't go. I love you.

(MURIEL runs into MR. P, breathless.)

MURIEL: Coco likes you. (She sits abruptly, pretending to read magazine.)

(KRISTAL walks in.)

KRISTAL: Hello Muriel. Hello Mrs. P. Oh your daughter called. She'll try to get in touch...uh...Sunday.

MRS. P: My daughter? Oh, my daughter. Thank you. OH THANK YOU!

MURIEL: (Rushes out.) Coco! Coco!

(MRS. P approaches the snoozing MR. P; YOUNG MRS. P approaches YOUNG MR. P.)

YOUNG MRS. P: (To MRS. P.) Even if you can stop him flirting in this room, there are too many rooms in this house.

MRS. P: (To MR. P.) You're mine because we have the same memories.

YOUNG MRS. P: (To YOUNG MR. P.) So why do you have to make everyone else so happy except for her? (Indicating MRS. P.)

(YOUNG MR. P and YOUNG MRS. P exit. MR. P awakes abruptly.)

MR. P: Mrs. Mrs. where are you?

(MRS. P rushes to him.)

MRS. P: What is it old man?

MR. P: I need to hold you. I'm frightened.

MRS. P: What are you frightened of?

MR. P: I need to hold you, so you won't fall down. Because you woke up scared.

MRS. P: I see. I see *(She helps him to chair.)* Today we're going on the balcony couch to sit. Do you hear? No more arguments. When you move to a different room, a lot of different things can happen. This chair is getting you down. Everybody needs a change.

MR. P: *(Turns resentful.)* Always bossing me around. You get out of here, old lady. I have things to do.

(MRS. P exits.)

SCENE: The past.

YOUNG MR. P: Hello.

YOUNG MRS. P: Hello.

YOUNG MR. P: How are you?

YOUNG MRS. P: Fine. How are you?

YOUNG MR. P: Top of my form. Top drawer. Never better.

YOUNG MRS. P: I'm busy working right now.

YOUNG MR. P: Oh I can see that all right, yes indeed I see that. Folding.

YOUNG MRS. P: I can't talk until after five. You know that.

YOUNG MR. P: I was wondering if you could come outside for just a minute. I have something to show you.

YOUNG MRS. P: To show me. Oh I couldn't, I just couldn't.

YOUNG MR. P: Sure you could. I'll get someone to watch these house dresses for a minute.

YOUNG MRS. P: You'll get me fired.

YOUNG MR. P: Then you'll marry me and have someone to take care of you.

YOUNG MRS. P: *(Flattered.)* Oh go away now.

YOUNG MR. P: OK if you won't come out I'll have to bring it in.

(YOUNG MRS. P busies herself folding. YOUNG MR. P signals at the door. In comes a string quartet playing "I'm in Love with You, Honey.")

SCENE: Room with a dais. Standing on platform are MR. P and MRS. P as in a tableau. MRS. P has a torn wedding veil on. MR. P has a cape around his shoulders. CHUCK is dancing around, directing the show.

CHUCK: Don't move Mr. P. This is a tableau. I got a piece of history here. You move to the right and put your arm around her. Now look stern. Remember, you are Goebbels and this here is Eva Braun. This is World War II, so look stern.

MR. P: I don't want to be Goebbels anymore.

MRS. P: Hush. It'll soon be tea time. Then you can rest. This is art. Isn't it, Chuck? Isn't this art?

CHUCK: With a capital R. Yessireebob. We'll get this little program together and then we need some explosives. Just a few. Nothing ostentatious. Then we'll bring World War II to a close.

MR. P: Will there be music? I like music.

CHUCK: Was the war to any particular tune you can think of?

MR. P: Over there. *(Sings.)* Over there...

CHUCK: *(Sings.)* And the caissons go rolling along...

MR. P: This robe itches.

CHUCK: It's the only one we could find.

MRS. P: What are my lines again?

CHUCK: I told you a hundred times. Do I have to write your lines down or something?

MRS. P: Well, some days I wake up and everything's fine. Then other days it all goes blank like you've pushed the button on the TV off. You know like the pictures are all there somewhere but they're not on the screen at all. Down below the box somewhere and if I could just push another button and bring them up—but there's no other button and—

CHUCK: Yeah yeah yeah. I'll write them down next time. You say "Hitler. I love you."

MRS. P: I love you? Are you sure that's what I'm supposed to say?

CHUCK: I wrote the play didn't I?

MRS. P: What am I doing with him, then, if I love Hitler?

CHUCK: Oh he's going to play both parts. Double up. Saves money.

MRS. P: Can I keep the veil after the show is over?

CHUCK: We'll see. You know it came out of the costume box and the nurse said we should share.

MRS. P: It does look nice on me.

MR. P: Very nice. Very very nice. I'm done. *(Shuffles off.)*

CHUCK: Actors can't leave until directors say they can. That's why actors are actors and directors are directors.

MR. P: I'm hungry *(Exits.)*

CHUCK: You're fired.

MRS. P: Who do I marry now?

CHUCK: Oh shut up. We were almost ready to take this to the other hall.

(YOUNG MR. P comes on stage. Enter YOUNG MRS. P, takes his arm.)

MRS. P: But you're just my memory. So go away. You don't belong here. This is no place for you. You're not allowed.

YOUNG MRS. P: And yet we stay.

YOUNG MR. P: We can't go away.

MRS. P: Why? It's so confusing here. What is real. The now they talk about won't stay.

(YOUNG MR. P and YOUNG MRS. P exit.)

MRS. P: I want to change the past. I've disappointed someone. Who could it be? *(Turns to ask them but they're gone.)*

(COCO and MURIEL walk through.)

MURIEL: I saw her. I saw her.

COCO: Who did you see? Did you see cook steal my Dodge Dart? It's nowhere to be seen. Did you see her?

MURIEL: Mrs. P.

COCO: Mrs. P stole my Dodge Dart?

MURIEL: No no—her daughter. I saw Mrs. P's daughter.

COCO: She just made that up.

MURIEL: Walking with Mrs. P chatting as nicely as you please.

COCO: And what did she look like then?

MURIEL: Well she was tall.

COCO: Yes.

MURIEL: Taller than I thought. And…

COCO: Yes? What?

MURIEL: She had on Kristal's shoes.

COCO: Are you sure?

MURIEL: I'm positive. I see them every day, don't I, sticking out in front of her. When we are in our circle.

COCO: Kristal's shoes. So she's a thief just like her mother.

MURIEL: Could be she stole your Dodge Dart too.

(YOUNG MRS. P and YOUNG MR. P enter stage, drift through. YOUNG MRS. P turns to MRS. P.)

YOUNG MRS. P: He must have thought me poor company because it turns out he'd flirt with a chair if it had a skirt on it.

(YOUNG MR. P turns to MR. P.)

YOUNG MR. P: The one she really loved never got off that bus. I learned that fast enough. She took my given name though, but did she ever love me?

(YOUNG MR. P and YOUNG MRS. P drift off.)

MR. P: *(Wakes.)* NO.

(Lights up. MRS. P rushes over.)

KRISTAL: You just upset him, Mrs. P. It's time to go now. We'll be taking you on a nice walk to the East Room, the one with the flowers on the wall.

(KRISTAL leads MRS. P reluctantly away.)

SCENE: MRS. P talking to DOCTOR.

MRS. P: Doctor that Mr. P over there—he held my hand yesterday. I mean he held my hand. *(Hastily adding.)* When now was yesterday.

DOCTOR: That's called affection for you, Mrs. P.

MRS. P: I wanted you to know something else.

DOCTOR: *(Impatient.)* Yes? Yes?

MRS. P: I like him so much but I'm afraid.

DOCTOR: Out with it, afraid?

MRS. P: I think he's losing his mind.

DOCTOR: You all are so you might as well shut up about it.

MRS. P: Oh I see. Old Timer's Disease?

DOCTOR: Perhaps. Alzheimer's yes.

MRS. P: Well we are old timers, that's true.

DOCTOR: Now's the time we hear your complaints, your questions. And what time is that?

MRS. P: Now.

DOCTOR: Yes, now.

(CHUCK enters, moves through office.)

CHUCK: *(To DOCTOR.)* I'm here to say I don't give a damn what day it is. The reason no one knows is because of you always telling us different days. It must be someone giving out bad dope. No two people in here have the same damn information. Something is wrong with the system. *(Exits.)*

SCENE: MURIEL approaches CHUCK.

MURIEL: I like your shirt, Chuck.

CHUCK: It's an artist's shirt.

MURIEL: Is it pure silk?

CHUCK: It used to be before I got in this place.

MURIEL: Could I touch it? Rub my hands down your pocket? Fold your collar? Um I love this shirt.

CHUCK: Take it. I have another one.

MURIEL: You really mean it?

(CHUCK strips to waist. Hands it over. MURIEL puts it on top of her dress.)

COCO: *(Storms in.)* What is going on here? You are half naked!

MURIEL: Chuck took the shirt right off his back to give to me. It still smells like him.

COCO: And where is mine?

CHUCK: I only wore one today.

COCO: It's not very polite, Chuck, to play favorites.

CHUCK: I always wear one shirt at a time.

COCO: Never mind. I'll go get your hairbrush. As a memento. I saw it in your room.

MURIEL: You were in his room?

CHUCK: You were in my room?

COCO: Only helping to straighten up the picture. I saw it was crooked on the wall.

CHUCK: You go in my room? That picture's of the Sixth Fleet. Not for women.

COCO: I'll just go up and get my souvenir. It looks like a silver hairbrush too. Thank you Chuck.

MURIEL: (*Stroking self.*) Thank you Chuck.

(*CHUCK left standing, looking after.*)

SCENE: KRISTAL with MR. P.

MR. P: No.

KRISTAL: Yes (*Holds up flash cards.*) Monday.

MR. P: Monday.

KRISTAL: Tuesday.

MR. P: No.

KRISTAL: Tuesday.

MR. P: Tuesday.

KRISTAL: Wednesday.

MR. P: No.

KRISTAL: Now we have Monday Tuesday, Wednesday.

MR. P: No Monday, No Tuesday, No Wednesday.

KRISTAL: Good.

MR. P: Where is Mrs. P? I've got to get her. I have something for her.

KRISTAL: We have Thursday and Friday left to read.

MR. P: The hell with them. Those days all smell the same around here. Soap and soup. *(Goes to empty chair.)* Mrs. P used to sit right over there. She had purple hair and the sun came in and sat on it sometimes and lit it up. She liked it here, crying the way she did. She must've liked it here to cry so much.

KRISTAL: She's in the new sunroom. Just for the morning. We're trying it out.

MR. P: No. She's the one with the days of the week and I'm not doing Thursday without her. Go get her. She dances with me. I think she's taken a fancy to me.

KRISTAL: Don't get excited. I'll call the doctor. *(Exits.)*

MR. P: NO. Get the purple lady back NOW.

SCENE: MRS. P is in her room, sorting photos.

MR. P: *(Enters.)* Hello. Hello. How are you?

MRS. P: Fine. How are you?

MR. P: I heard you were in a new place with flowers on the wall. The damn ivy on the wall here follows my every move.

MRS. P: Well I'm sure you're up to your old tricks and now you don't have to watch out for me watching you all the time.

MR. P: Oh applesauce.

MRS. P: What do you want?

MR. P: I—I was lonely.

MRS. P: Call a temp.

MR. P: No, really lonely.

MRS. P: What are you looking at?

MR. P: These pictures.

MRS. P: Our daughter.

MR. P: I don't have a daughter.

MRS. P: Well I do.

MR. P: Hey Mrs.

MRS. P: What old man?

MR. P: I miss Bing Crosby. Don't you? I really really miss the way he'd sing, don't you? Would you dance with me?

(MRS. P hesitates, puts down photos. Goes to him. COCO and MURIEL poke heads in door.)

COCO: Yoo hoo!

MURIEL: Mr. P, Coco likes you a lot.

(All freeze. Enter KRISTAL. Pulls COCO and MURIEL aside.)

KRISTAL: Mr. and Mrs. P are trying to be alone, ladies. Come with me.

MURIEL: Oh Kristal, we were just talking about you. Well, not me of course, but some of the others in the craft room.

COCO: I'll do it.

MURIEL: I never get to.

COCO: If you are—

MURIEL: *(Blurts.)* If you are a virgin.

KRISTAL: Why Coco, that's a personal question. Why do you ask such a thing?

MURIEL: Being a nurse and all.

COCO: Quiet Muriel!

MURIEL: I told them that remark "dirty nurse" wasn't funny, even though I know you have to wash other people's—uh... feet.

SCENE: *YOUNG MRS. P is packing her suitcase when YOUNG MR. P arrives.*

YOUNG MR. P: Where are you going?

YOUNG MRS. P: Away.

YOUNG MR. P: For good?

YOUNG MRS. P: You and your floozies.

YOUNG MR. P: You going to him?

YOUNG MRS. P: It's just a place to go.

YOUNG MR. P: Not this time. One more chance. *(Tries to hug her.)* I brought you a present *(Runs to door, brings in phonograph.)* No one dances like us. We're what we have. What else is there? *(Scrambling.)* We're the ones who say "Do you want donuts or toast in the morning."

YOUNG MRS. P: Hold the toast or have it with Camille. I can't break you of it.

(Back to present. YOUNG MRS. P leads MRS. P to corner of room. YOUNG MR. P leads MR. P to MRS. P.)

MR. P: *(Sidles up.)* I'm in the mood for spooning.

LOUDSPEAKER: *(Voiceover.)* All attendants to nurses' station.

(Enter MURIEL.)

MURIEL: Somebody's dead. I saw the doctor carry him out. It was Wing 300. Chuck.

MRS. P: Chuck!?

MURIEL: Let me go back for a minute and check. Somebody can get his fedora if they're quick. There's a fedora in his room. I saw it. I think it was a hat, anyway.

COCO: He was always poor company anyway.

MURIEL: Who?

COCO: Whoever it was who died.

MRS. P: They let people die here?

MR. P: That's just scare talk. Get out of here. Both of you. *(Turns to MRS. P.)* Now this is to make you perk up a little. You've been so mopey of late.

(MRS. P softens. MR. P dumps photos on floor and takes shoebox.)

MR. P: This here box plays a tune and when you die, I'm going to bury it in the ground on your grave so when anybody steps on it, it plays our song, and you think of me and no one else.

(MRS. P takes box gently.)

MR. P: Do you like it?

MRS. P: I do. I like it a lot. *(Places lid on top. Lifts lid up and down.)* Where's the music?

MR. P: You ain't dead yet!

MRS. P: You're a cutup. I like that in a man.

MR. P: Come here. Look at the sun on the venetian blinds this time of day.

(MRS. P goes over. He grabs a kiss.)

MR. P: You make a body feel different. Real different. Will you tell them to let you back in my day room? I won't yell anymore. I promise.

SCENE: Lights up. YOUNG MRS. P sitting up sleeping with bandages around wrists. YOUNG MR. P enters. Kisses her. Put coat around her.

YOUNG MR. P: I'm taking you home. I won't yell anymore. I promise.

YOUNG MRS. P: I want to go home too.

MRS. P: When I woke up all my clothes were ruined on the floor with the water. The cat had no food. I had to open an old sandwich to find a piece of meat. The baby had been living without a taste of fruit. The counters on my sink were dirty. The people were having a meeting in my house. I couldn't get inside to clean it. Who's taking care of my kitchen now?

ACT 2

MR. P is in sunroom deconstructing window area. Enter COCO and MURIEL excitedly. MR. P crams paper in his pocket.

COCO: *(To MURIEL.)* You must believe me. Muriel, the new doctor is after me. I swear before the gods in the heavens, he wants my body. He says he wants to… *(Lowers voice.)* examine me. I think I know where.

MURIEL: He seems like a nice young man to me.

COCO: Watch out. They're the ones who'll fool you. He probably wants to violate me.

MURIEL: Oh dear. Should we report him?

COCO: Who to? They're all in cahoots.

MURIEL: What did he say, dear? The new doctor.

COCO: *(Shouting.)* He said "I want to examine you."

MURIEL: What?

COCO: Examine— here, *(Looks around for paper.)* I'll write it. *(Grabs paper sticking out of MR. P's pocket. Grabs crayon. Scribbles.)*

MURIEL: You want to examine me?

COCO: No, I'm trying to tell you what the man said to me. He wants to violate me.

MURIEL: *(Gasps.)* No. Mr. P?

MR. P: *(Comes over. Grabs paper from MURIEL.)* This is mine! Get your own paper.

COCO: But I'm trying to tell Muriel something.

MURIEL: She wants to violate me?

MRS. P: *(Enters.)* Why is Muriel crying, Coco? What have you done now? I'm calling the doctor.

COCO: No. Don't do that. Not him.

(COCO rushes out with MURIEL following. MR. P storms over to MRS. P.)

MR. P: They took my paper. *(Shows her. Stuffs back in pocket.)*

MRS. P: Turn it over. What is it?

MR. P: It's mine.

MRS. P: Give it here. Give it now!

(MR. P reluctantly hands it over.)

MRS. P: *(Reads.)* I want to examine you. Coco gave you this?

MR. P: It was my paper.

MRS. P: Coco again... I knew it ! Kristal! Nurse!

(MR. P goes back to crayon on the wall. MRS. P leads MR. P to chair, takes his crayons.)

MR. P: I'm glad to see you, lady, where have you been? I have something for you. *(He pulls a piece of squashed cake wrapped in a napkin from his pocket.)* For you.

MRS. P: For me?

MR. P: Yep. I saved my extra dessert for you I did and pulled it right off the table—for you.

MRS. P: I don't know what to say. Well thank you.

MR. P: I've taken a leaning to you.

MRS. P: A leaning?

MR. P: Yes. I realized when you left to go to that other room—the one with the leaves and pictures on the wall—that I'd taken a shine to you.

MRS. P: That pleases me.

MR. P: That's why... *(Indicates cake.)*

MRS. P: Thank you.

MR. P: I'd like to say something and I've been practicing it. So here it goes. I don't want you in the other sunroom anymore and that's why, *(Gets down on one knee.)* I'd like to ask you to be my holy wedded wife.

MRS. P: *(Startled.)* Oh.

MR. P: Don't you want to?

MRS. P: Well you take my breath away. I don't know what to say. I just came in to do these flashcards. (Shows him.) Thursday, Friday, Saturday was for today and I'm—I'm quite taken aback.

MR. P: Well you don't have to answer right away. You could tell me after supper.

MRS. P: Early seating?

MR. P: Or late. I'm not rushing you.

MRS. P: I see.

MR. P: We could walk around the patio together every day and in this way we could get along.

MRS. P: That's true. We could.

MR. P: It's just you and me and nobody needs to know if you want to keep a secret.

MRS. P: Well, what would I wear?

MR. P: We'll think of that later. A nightgown?

MRS. P: Oh no we know each other much too well for that.

MR. P: I like the way your hair looks when you sit by the window. I'd like to make you stay by the window a while more so I got this idea. To be mine forever more.

MRS. P: That's a long time.

MR. P: It's just the amount of time you got left. That's all it is and always has been. You're not spoke for, are you?

MRS. P: (Huffy.) Why of course not. What kind of a woman do you think I am?

MR. P: Now calm yourself. I know you don't go from room to room. You're not that kind of woman. I can tell.

MRS. P: Well what would we do if we were married?

MR. P: That's not the point I'm making. We'd be together all the time and they couldn't separate us when we were working up to a good fight and you'd do my day cards and not that stupid nurse. Say yes, please and we'll have a celebration.

(CHUCK enters, bustling.)

CHUCK: Hello folks. Today we're all going to get up on the stage and do a tableau. We're going to say something about this place we live in and when we get it down pat we'll call in the bigwigs that own the place and sell it to them. And then they'll pay us. I used to be in PR and this is exactly the way to do it.

MR. P: Excuse me, but the Mrs. and I were having a personal conversation.

CHUCK: Save it for later, bud. This is a money-making proposition and I know the deal. *(Calls.)* Come in! Come in!

(COCO and MURIEL come in.)

CHUCK: Sit down. Sit down. We're doing a little blue-skying. We're going to do a little publicity for the docs and try to bring in a little business for ourselves. Sit. Sit. I've run these sessions before so I'll just sit you all here and you tell me the first thing that pops out of your mind. And I'll try to get it on tape. *(Picks up vase.)* Speak right up. This is just a little jocular levity. It's not a loudspeaker. We'll make a mint. Wouldn't you all like a few extra smackers?

MURIEL: Chuck's dead. I saw them take him out of Wing 300.

CHUCK: I'm Chuck.

MURIEL: Then it must have been Wing 400.

CHUCK: Well that was a lousy thing to do to mess up our session.

(Silence.)

CHUCK: We need to think up some slogans and get some respect around here—get more attention. Better food. More nurses.

MURIEL: These maids are nurses?

COCO: These are not maids, Muriel. This is not the Plaza.

CHUCK: Well, take it up later. Now lie a little and make this place sound good. Get it on the billboards and then we'll get more field trips like we used to.

MRS. P: The ice skating rink. We went there to a show, I always wanted to be a figure skater.

COCO: *(Snickering.)* You have to have a figure first. Not just padding.

CHUCK: Shut up you ladies. I'll go first. "Pinecrest Rest Haven"... later we could add some music to it... *(Looks out window. To MR. P dozing.)* Wake up, bud... "Pinecrest is well situated." See? Like that. How do you like it?

MRS. P: Well I don't know. What does it mean... Pinecrest is well situated?

CHUCK: It sits well. Like here on a hill.

MURIEL: No skyscrapers?

CHUCK: Of course there's no skyscrapers in Florida.

MRS. P: This is Florida?

CHUCK: I give up. You can't do this simple thing. I'll go somewhere else. *(Gets up to leave.)*

MR. P: The chairs are nice. *(Settles back to sleep.)*

CHUCK: *(Turns back.)* I like that. "Pinecrest Rest Haven. The chairs are nice." I like that.

(MRS. P is beaming. Freeze scene.)

SCENE: YOUNG MRS. P in apron; MR. P comes home.

YOUNG MR. P: Where's my kitty kat?

YOUNG MRS. P: *(Pretending.)* Who is it?

YOUNG MR. P: Me. Bumberchuck.

YOUNG MRS. P: Bumberchuck who?

YOUNG MR. P: I brought you something. *(Goes to door and hauls in basket with champagne, flowers, candles. Unpacking them.)* It happened. It happened with a bang. First Vice President in charge of sales for the Central Mountain Region of the US of A.

YOUNG MRS. P: I can't believe it finally happened.

YOUNG MR. P: Why not?

(He sweeps her up and dances her across the room in an old-fashioned cheek to cheek. Twirls her around.)

YOUNG MRS. P: *(Makes telephone ringing sound with her lips.)* Brrrrnnng brrrrnnng.

(YOUNG MR. P falls in with the game.)

YOUNG MRS. P: The telephone. It's for you.

(YOUNG MR. P drops to his knees. She leans over. His ear is pressed against her breast.)

YOUNG MRS. P: It's for you!

YOUNG MR. P: Hello? Hello? Who is this please?

YOUNG MRS. P: It's me.

YOUNG MR. P: I can't talk now. I got places to be, people to see.

YOUNG MRS. P: It's me.

YOUNG MR. P: Hello? I can't hear you. Hello in there? Hello? Speak up please.

YOUNG MRS. P: *(Jumps up.)* It's time. It's time. *(She runs to a box. Opens it. Puts mirror on table.)* It must be a terrible thing to have a poor memory.

YOUNG MR. P: Yes baby, you said it.

YOUNG MRS. P: To not have any celebrations, none! *(Puts on lipstick.)*

YOUNG MR. P: *(Combs hair before mirror.)* To have days without dancing and without end...like some people...like the guys I work with, for instance.

YOUNG MRS. P: It's a terrible thing to have a marriage without dancing.

YOUNG MR. P: Well we can't mourn for others.

YOUNG MRS. P: *(Puts on skirt, beads.)* Maybe the others would want to dance but they just have a poor memory.

YOUNG MR. P: Maybe.

YOUNG MRS. P: *(Lets her hair down.)* Maybe love is having a good memory. Remembering all the steps.

YOUNG MR. P: And the twirls. Don't forget what I told you last night. The left foot. Up. It can never be too high.

YOUNG MRS. P: *(Puts on her shoes.)* I know. I know. You are right. I saw that. Never high enough.

YOUNG MR. P: *(Brushes shoulders with clothes brush.)* One should not be afraid of a routine.

YOUNG MRS. P: Or lift a leg high enough. I remember everything you say. We'll be great tonight.

YOUNG MR. P: Nobody would ever be able to do it with me like you. That's for sure. *(Shines shoes.)* When the lights go on in that contest—well we'd better start practicing our bow.

YOUNG MRS. P: *(Applying makeup.)* You'd never be able to start again, would you. Once you get a partner with a good routine and she knows how to lift together with you—to rise and lower and never fall—that is a very important thing. I feel sorry. Some people don't have it at all.

YOUNG MR. P: Some people don't have the gift of dance, a song, or taps on their shoes, much less a beautiful partner.

YOUNG MRS. P: Who lifts her leg up in the air real well in the back. Right? Like you want me to. For you.

YOUNG MR. P: They're ready, honey. Don't make us fail. They'll pay good money to see this famous team. *(Escorts her on his arm around the stage in a promenade.)* This gentleman in the front says he sent you a fan letter. Did you ever receive such a thing in the mail?

YOUNG MRS. P: Is the gentleman a count from Italy? Did he fall in love with me because of my last film?

YOUNG MR. P: Right. See sir? Never be of little faith with the great or near great.

(They twirl and spin and dip. YOUNG MR. P gets a glass off the table. Gives one to her. Clicks glass. Makes a toast to imaginary audience.)

YOUNG MR. P: Ladies and gentlemen. You may have thought we were just two losers but it's not the end of the race until you are number one. And tonight we celebrate. It's what you do with what you have left. When the other guy drops back.

YOUNG MRS. P: And we are out in front. Mister First Vice President and his wife. *(Makes a bow.)*

YOUNG MR. P: You have to know when to hold and know when to fold.

(Phone rings. Magic stops.)

YOUNG MR. P: *(Answers.)* Hello? Hello? I can't hear you. Who is there? Yes, that's my name. Yes, We have a daughter. Fran... Yes. No no NO... *(Drops glass.)*

(YOUNG MRS. P rushes over. YOUNG Mr. P drops phone.)

YOUNG MR. P: It's our Fran. *(Picks phone up.)* An accident.

(Back to present day at Pinecrest. Everyone except MR. P and MRS. P has gone.)

MR. P: *(Voiceover.)* It's what you do with what you have left.

MR. P: *(Sleeping. Starts abruptly.)* NO!

(MRS. P rushes to him.)

MR. P: What do we do now? *(Head in hands.)*

MRS. P: We have tea unless we've missed it already. Unless the tearoom is empty. *(She tidies up, takes off her scarf, dusting, humming, fluffing pillows.)*

MR. P: I was dreaming of Fran...

MRS. P: *(Stops.)* I don't know Fran.

MR. P: I thought so. I thought we both did together.

MRS. P: Fran became an angel. Suddenly, she became an angel and that's that. *(She stops keeping house and sinks in chair, numb and dazed.)*

SCENE: COCO sees CHUCK and goes to him with a present wrapped in newspaper.

CHUCK: What's this?

COCO: An offering.

CHUCK: What's an offering?

COCO: An offering of love from me to you. A token. If I liked you and I'm not saying that I do, but if I did, I'd give you something as a token but I'm not sure what you would think if I did.

CHUCK: *(Opens present.)* It's a goddamn picture.

COCO: Yes.

CHUCK: Of who?

COCO: Of me.

CHUCK: Of you?

COCO: When I was young. For you to remember me by.

CHUCK: Why the hell would I want to do that?

MURIEL: So here you are.

COCO: Can't I have a moment's peace without you?

MURIEL: But you are my girlfriend.

(KRISTAL walks through. CHUCK begins to follow her.)

KRISTAL: No, I can't. I already told you.

CHUCK: But it's a different machine this time. This one has two plugs, one for each person, guaranteed to make them fall in love. I'm unveiling it Thursd—

KRISTAL: NO! I said NO! Oh I'm sorry. I'm so sorry, no, I mean I can't. I... Sorry.

SCENE: DOCTOR and MRS. P.

DOCTOR: This record says you and Mr. P have been married fifty-four years.

MRS. P: Well I have. He hasn't always been.

DOCTOR: And that your only child is dead.

MRS. P: No she's not dead. She's just not alive.

DOCTOR: And it says here you won't admit it.

MRS. P: She's coming on Sunday.

DOCTOR: And Mr. P?

MRS. P: Who?

DOCTOR: The old man you take care of.

MRS. P: Oh him.

DOCTOR: You love him.

MRS. P: No I hate him but when I meet him again I love him.

DOCTOR: Why?

MRS. P: Oh he isn't trustworthy. He has never been worthy of my trust.

DOCTOR: How?

MRS. P: He cheats and lies and spends all my money and pretends we're not married.

DOCTOR: But yet you stay in the same recreation room when you could be happier in another place. We offered you a new facility with new friends.

MRS. P: Oh I couldn't do that. And leave my new friend Mr. P, the old man. He seems to like me and I like him. I'm all he has. I am his past. If I remember something and I left him I'd have to take it with me, then what would he do without it.

DOCTOR: He'd have the present. Which is right now. That's all. Good food, good rest, friends, recreation, but right now.

MRS. P: Oh I couldn't take his memories away and I'm the only one who owns them. I'm what he has left. That wouldn't be fair. I love him.

DOCTOR: Get yourself together. Right now! Do you hear me?

(CHUCK still following KRISTAL. CHUCK turns away at the sight of the DOCTOR. KRISTAL enters, observing. MRS. P puts her head on her arms on the desk.)

DOCTOR: I guess you should get another profession, Kristal. This one isn't working out for anybody.

KRISTAL: I'll be leaving at the end of the month. I've made my mind up once and for all.

DOCTOR: You say that every month, Kristal. For God's sake leave, before they take your blood with them when they do. It's all too hard. Save something, Kristal, like yourself. Just leave.

KRISTAL: (Goes to MRS. P.) And what of Mrs. P?

DOCTOR: She's faking, you know.

(KRISTAL helps MRS. P to her feet.)

KRISTAL: (Looks into MRS. P's face.) Only on a good day...a very good day.

(KRISTAL leads MRS. P out.)

SCENE: MRS. P., COCO, and MURIEL in sitting room.

COCO: I'm just here for a while. Just to do research. I've always wanted to find the truth in a situation such as this—to reach into the soul of any environment. Those people in their chairs.

MRS. P: Some days I wake up so lonely I ask them for a pill—I want my mother or my baby. I want something I can't name.

I feel everything has died and I'm the only thing left. Please don't think I'm not grateful. I'm not on the streets like some old ladies. There's enough to eat here, and all the toilet paper you can use.

COCO: I am a good investigative reporter. For instance, when someone soiled the couch over there—It was the middle pillow—well everyone was happy to avoid the stain—or turn the cushion. Everyone pretended no one had shit on the couch.

MURIEL: The commissary is only open two hours a day and there's nothing in it. If I could spend one hour shopping the way I used to, I'd never pass the time of day with the likes of these people again.

COCO: About that stain on the couch—I said "Coco. Pretend this is a top story to go to the late edition," and I followed my nose to the laundry room. I finally found out who did it. But then he died. My whole day wasted.

MURIEL: What I wouldn't give for an intelligent conversation about necklaces—with a thoughtful person who could talk about fashions.

COCO: However, the fabric has been replaced. Now it's apple green as you can see. Colors! Now that would make a wonderful memoir.

MRS. P: I want my own plant in the window again—and to lay my own table with yellow dishes. Sometimes I close my eyes and imagine my old house. It always smelled like sausage or dust in the attic—where do those smells go? Or are they still there in someone else's house?

(Enter CHUCK with a ukulele.)

CHUCK: OK girls, get up. I've got three umbrellas and a chair and a routine that kept me up all night. No ordinaries today. We can get this show on the road in one hour flat. Coco—you're short—

COCO: Petite.

CHUCK: You be in front. Mrs. P next and Muriel in the back. It's going to be called "A Day in Pinecrest," us arriving all in a row. They'll love it. Get UP. Do you want to sleep away your life till you're in a dirt sleep?

(The women stay slumped in their chairs. Reluctantly, they take umbrellas from CHUCK and line up. He pulls out a folding chair to show how he'd like them to pivot the chair while holding an umbrella, then sits in it.)

CHUCK: There. Any questions, girls?

MRS. P: Chuck, I have a question.

CHUCK: Yes yes.

MRS. P: How do I make Mr. P not lonely?

CHUCK: Bad doesn't get better, Dolly. Now get back in line and show a bit of leg, won't you? The audience paid to see a little privilege. Hope and energy, girls, that's what we give them.

(No one moves.)

COCO: I'm not playing. I am an intellectual. I don't dance.

SCENE: Lights flashing. Sirens.

LOUDSPEAKER: *(Voiceover.)* ALERT FOURTH FLOOR.

(MR. P is lying on the floor with all around him. MRS. P enters center door. Two attendants are YOUNG MR. P and YOUNG MRS. P. The following lines are spoken slowly as MRS. P moves from bravado to breaking.)

MRS. P: Let me through. He's just trying to get my attention again. I know him like a book.

(They stretcher him.)

MRS. P: Let me go. He's just doing this to get on my good side.

(Exit stretcher.)

MRS. P: That man will do anything to be in the center. It's just an April fool joke.

CHUCK: Are you crying because he was mean to you?

MRS. P: No, because he was nice to me.

CHUCK: You can sit by me for lunch.

MRS. P: No, he must just be having a bad day.

CHUCK: Here's my card. I throw a good funeral. *(Hands her his card. Shrugs.)*

DOCTOR: Mrs. P. Where are you?

MRS. P: *(Numbly.)* Here.

DOCTOR: Where is here?

MRS. P: With you.

DOCTOR: And what month is it, Mrs. P?

MRS. P: April. April 20.

DOCTOR: Yes. That's right!

MRS. P: *(Alarmed that she gave the right answer.)* Oh no. I think Christmas time is near. I feel that. It's close to the holidays, maybe Thanksgiving.

DOCTOR: I think you were right the first time, Mrs. P, and I think you know it and I know it and I think I know why. You're afraid we'll send you to another home. That we'll send you elsewhere.

MRS. P: Where is elsewhere?

(YOUNG MRS. P enters.)

YOUNG MRS. P: *(To MRS. P.)* If you don't want to leave Mr. P alone, you'd better be more alert next time.

MRS. P: *(To YOUNG MRS. P.)* I know. I know. I was just so very tired for a moment.

DOCTOR: Excuse me?

YOUNG MRS. P: You'll never get more in here from him than you got out there.

MRS. P: *(To YOUNG MRS. P.)* Can you stay with me? If Mr. P leaves?

DOCTOR: A little while. I could stay a little while.

YOUNG MR. P: Not for long. You know that. My time here is short.

DOCTOR: I haven't much time you know.

MRS. P: I know that.

(YOUNG MR. P approaches. YOUNG MRS. P takes his arm.)

MRS. P: But you're just my memory. So go away. You don't belong here. This is no place for you. You're not allowed.

YOUNG MRS. P: And yet we stay.

YOUNG MR. P: We can't go away.

MRS. P: Why? It's so confusing here. What is real? The now they talk about won't stay.

YOUNG MR. P: The past becomes now.

MRS. P: I wanted to change the past but it all went away before I could get to it.

(All file in, joining MRS. P, to form a group.)

DOCTOR: *(To MURIEL.)* Where is Coco?

MURIEL: It's a surprise.

DOCTOR: She's late.

MURIEL: She's not coming, but I'm sworn to secrecy.

DOCTOR: Is she ill?

MURIEL: Oh no, never better.

(COCO appears at center door, wearing a hat and gloves, and carrying a suitcase.)

COCO: Here I am.

DOCTOR: So you are.

MURIEL: Somebody's dead.

DOCTOR: Quiet Muriel.

MRS. P: Is he still dead?

MURIEL: Oh yes, quite. They took him out.

COCO: Shut up Muriel. This is my moment. You all may have noticed my traveling garb.

MRS. P: Yes. It doesn't match at all. A green scarf would pick it up.

COCO: Will you close your trap for five minutes or I'll hit you with my pocketbook.

MRS. P: Purse. Purse. Yours is a purse.

MURIEL: Go ahead, Coco, tell them why you have your coat on.

COCO: I'm leaving.

DOCTOR: You're leaving? Where are you going?

COCO: My son is coming for me and I'll be living with him from now on.

DOCTOR: Is that so?

COCO: Yes, I'll be doing a major American newsletter—research, writing, folding—

MURIEL: Mailing.

COCO: *(Hisses.)* Quiet. This is mine.

MRS. P: 'Bye Coco.

CHUCK: Goodbye Coco, I don't need you in my routine anyway.

MRS. P: People who leave die.

MURIEL: Let's see what's in your suitcase.

COCO: Excuse me, there's my cab. *(Exits.)*

(DOCTOR hurries out after her.)

MURIEL: There's nothing in her suitcase. I looked in the hallway.

MRS. P: *(Calls out after her.)* You forgot your PURSE. It's here on the chair. *(Throws it out after her.)*

LOUDSPEAKER: *(Voiceover.)* Pill time.

SCENE: Lights up on MR. P, snoozing center bench—front stage in front of curtain—with oxygen tank at his side, tubes in his nose. YOUNG MR. P and YOUNG MRS. P move from opposite sides to greet each other.

YOUNG MRS. P: Hello.

YOUNG MR. P: Hello.

YOUNG MRS. P: How are you?

YOUNG MR. P: Never better. And you?

YOUNG MRS. P: Fine. Fine.

(MRS. P enters. She is wearing slippers and robe, disheveled. YOUNG MR. P and YOUNG MRS. P lead her to MR. P's bench. She sits. They stand behind.)

MRS. P: Hello.

MR. P: Hello.

MRS. P: They are still serving tea.

MR. P: With honey?

(MRS. P nods.)

MR. P: And hot milk? I'd like that.

MRS. P: With me?

MR. P: You're the one I want for tea time.

MRS. P: So you're my date. Now you're mine?

MR. P: I was already yours. Are you new here? I like your hair. I love red hair. I've seen you here before.

MRS. P: I didn't know you noticed me.

MR. P: How could I not notice you. Your heart is in my chest with your name on it.

MRS. P: What does it say?

MR. P: Oh... ah... you know... *(Points to his chest.)* your name.

MRS. P: Mr., it's all gone now. This is what we got.

MR. P: What does that mean?

MRS. P: Now or then. It's all the same to me.

MR. P: What does *now* look like?

MRS. P: Oh it's real pretty. Like real fancy wallpaper with roses.

MR. P: I always think heaven may be behind those roses on the wall.

YOUNG MRS. P: *(To MR. P.)* It's time to go.

MRS. P: Wait wait. I got us matching Pinecrest hats from the commissary.

(MR. P does not take the hat. MR. P stands. MRS. P starts to stand. YOUNG MRS. P and YOUNG MR. P lead him gently off. YOUNG MRS. P's arm is linked to MR. P. His apparatus is left behind on the floor. Light on his empty place on the bench widens to include MRS. P on the bench. She rises as if to follow them. YOUNG MR. P turns back, returns to MRS. P. Sits by MRS. P, as YOUNG MRS. P leads MR. P off.)

YOUNG MR. P: *(To MRS. P.)* It's time to stay.

(He sits by her, takes her hand. She leans her head on his shoulder. He stands, takes her hand. They dance to "I'm in Love with You, Honey.")

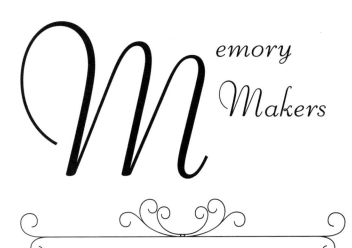

THE POET AND THE POEM
INTERVIEWS

Robert Pinsky was born in Long Branch, New Jersey, on October 20, 1940, and is a poet, essayist, and translator. From 1997 to 2000, he served as United States Poet Laureate at the Library of Congress. He is the author of ten collections of poetry, most recently, *At the Foundling Hospital*; as well as numerous collections of essays and a verse translation of Dante's *Inferno*. Pinsky is a professor of English and creative writing in the graduate writing program at Boston University. This interview was recorded at the Library of Congress in 1996 and was nationally broadcast.

Robert Pinsky

GRACE: Poet and critic Robert Pinsky is enjoying celebration of a new book, a verse translation of *The Inferno* of Dante, a beautiful book. It's being heralded by the literary world and recently won the Los Angeles book award, which is...?

ROBERT: The award is the Los Angeles Times Book Prize in Poetry.

GRACE: I want to stay with your Dante for a moment because it's an occasion in literature. And the first thing I want to know is, how did you get the idea that you wanted to do this? At what point in your life did you know that you were going to do this?

ROBERT: Well, it started with an assignment. It would be nice to tell you I had a profound attachment to *The Inferno* and I did have a great teacher, one of the great critics of the twentieth century when I was in college, Francis Fergusson, author of *The Idea of a Theater*. He wrote a book about purgatory, *The Purgatorio*; I read it. He introduced me to Dante, but it was, what, about twenty or twenty-five years later that my then-publisher put together a book with twenty different poets, each doing a canto or two. And I fell in love with the technical challenge, the technical problem of doing an English *terza rima* which was supposed to be impossible, and there is something attractive about it. So I did Canto 28 for that assignment, and somebody couldn't do Canto 20, and I did Canto 20—and sort of secretly to amuse myself the way people play computer games or do crossword puzzles—I started to do Canto 1 because it was hard to stop, and when I finished Canto 1, I realized I was starting something. I started thinking about the math. Well three cantos, that's a tenth of the road almost, and then I sat down with some friends, sat down with my friend Seamus Heaney, who had already done a couple of them, and talked about it and decided I would go ahead and do it all. So on some level it was chance, and a kind of technical, I don't know the word to use for it, "puzzle-solving appeal." I think the more profound aspects of the project may have been working on me unconsciously, but consciously it was the combination of chance—and the love of difficulty that makes people do things. Everybody loves difficulty. You know people make a lot of money in this country. Athletes, football or basketball stars, for instance, the first thing they do is learn how to play golf, or kids compete in video arcades, and that fascination with what's difficult really was the beginning of the project.

GRACE: Let us talk about your use of American history. I'm thinking of your poem about the Triangle Fire, "Shirt." Using history as poetry. What made you decide to separate the poem into its elements like cloth—as a fabric itself which would come apart? What possessed you? How did that fall?

ROBERT: Well, the poem began, as poems often do, with the sounds of the words. I was really just thinking about old sewing machines, treadle-operated sewing machines and how beautiful they are, you know the gilt engraving on the arm, the black arm with gold engraving on it and the wrought-iron treadle and the wooden platform with the black steel that fits in sort of neatly, and it was the sound of needle, bobbin, treadle, union, those parts of the thing. But at the time I wrote the poem, I was thinking a lot about creation, which is one of the subjects of this book, *The Want Bone*. It's largely about making, which is also destroying. Civilization in all of its horror and ugliness and its beauty consists of—you know, it's really all the work of Shiva, the Hindu goddess with the hammer who makes and breaks any artifact you look at. I was thinking at the time I wrote this poem about the idea that any artifact you look at—could one understand its history—even a word, if you think of a word as an artifact—could one understand its history and all the human ingenuity and resourcefulness and suffering and agony that went into it, you could recreate the history of the whole world from it, if you could understand it.

And the poem flowed out of the sounds of those words, and in its flowing it went into the channels of the conscious thinking I'd been doing about creation. I'd been thinking a lot about religion; I'm not a practicing anything. I don't practice any, but I'm interested in religion and certain religions, as one of the great, great episodes in the history of creativity or creation.

GRACE: You have been called "anecdotal," you've been called "discursive," you've been called "august," you've been called "neoclassic." You have been called "narrative," "natural." I see all this very much balanced within your work. But I'm curious about how you describe yourself. Of course, we're all many things, so why can't you be those many things. But if someone were to say: "well, just what kind of poetry do you write," how would you describe your voice?

ROBERT: I think the kind of poetry I write is, I think, about the whole range of things that people call poetry or work. I suppose that more than most I'm very attached to the old, old roots of poetry as a bodily art, that I'm very given to the old, old traditions of the sounds of poetry. And that I think of it as the most bodily of all the arts. Even more bodily than dance, because in dance the medium is the body of an expert, of an artist, but in poetry the medium is the body of the *audience*, the medium is the column of air shaped into meaning—sounds in the mouth of anybody at all. And that's probably kind of an archaic and ancient idea of poetry. There are people who are interested in other things, but for me the core of it is that air inside a body. I'm very interested in memorization, which is the process of incorporating a poem. So I would say the kind of poetry I write is the kind that emphasizes the physical qualities of the words.

GRACE: You've just changed my mind. I was thinking that poetry wasn't able to do what Cleo Laine did yesterday. I heard her hit a G above a high C and I thought, now we just never can get that high. We just can never belt it out quite like that. It's just on the page and a poem doesn't do that. And you're saying "oh yes, it comes through the body, oh yes." You can do a G above high C and you don't have to be schooled in a conservatory. So I'm taking what you say now as true, and happy about it, because I was just thinking a little about limitations yesterday. So you make the poem everybody's property.

ROBERT: Well, a great singer or a great dancer is an artist and an athlete and that art is physical or bodily in that sense, but if I recite a poem by Yeats or Frost to myself or an Emily Dickinson, I'm not a great athlete. I didn't write the words. But the actual physical forming of the words that was choreographed and determined by that now-dead artist inhabits my body. If I say "Once out of nature I shall never take / My bodily form from any natural thing. / But such a form as Grecian goldsmiths make / Of hammered gold and gold enameling / To keep a drowsy emperor awake," etc., if I do a long sentence like that, it's not an athletic feat like hitting a high G. Not to say that hitting a high G is only an athletic feat. I hope it was a feat of expression by Cleo Laine as well. But the feat is the feat of Yeats or Dickinson or, God knows, of Chaucer, inhabiting a body that is perhaps hundreds of years in the future or is thousands of miles distant and that is a body art. It's a bodily feat. You know my lips and my tongue and my teeth and my breath are performing that work of art. "While that my soul repairs to her devotion, / Here I entomb my flesh, that it betimes / May take acquaintance of this heap of dust, / To which the blast of Death's incessant motion, / Fed with the exhalation of our crimes, / Drives all at last." That was a little bit of the bodily configuration of sounds determined by George Herbert in the seventeenth century in England, and that refined and aristocratic Englishman actually determined what the body of the grandchild of Jewish immigrants speaking the English of twentieth-century America would do, you know, two hundred and fifty years later. It's extraordinary and it's not physical in the way that the high G is physical, but it's physical in a way that's more intimate.

GRACE: Now there is a new book before us which will be coming out very soon, and it is *The Figured Wheel: New and Collected Poems 1966–1996*. *The Want Bone* you describe as having a theme, maybe a premise, which is creation and destruction. Would you say that even though these are disparate poems put together, there's something you see that is alike about all of them?

ROBERT: Yeah, I'm very interested in a subject that I don't know the name for, civilization or culture or history... all have some kind of drawback to them. But I'm interested in the way we dress and the movies we watch and the crimes we commit. The nicknames that torturers have for different kinds of torture. The heroic couplet, jazz choruses, what musicians call the rhythm changes. I've got rhythm changes, all these makings, and it's how they fit together. As I look back on my work or think about my childhood, I've always been interested in how people do that. I can remember in grade school watching movies about the glass-making industry or the paper industry or oil refining—I guess corporations used to give them to the schools for free. I can remember watching those complicated machines make those things and think, "You know, when all the grown-ups die off and it's our turn, we are not going to be able to work, nobody's going to learn how to do that. I know these kids can't do that. These kids are not going to learn how to do all that." I would get anxious that we certainly were not going to have paper after a while because those machines were clearly too complicated for anybody to learn how to work them, amongst the people I knew, the kids I knew. And that may have been stupid, as it was. As a thought, it may have been a premature aspect of my wonder at the way all these things do fit together or fail to fit together. I mean, to some extent that's true. If you look at what a downtown in a typical American small city or town was in 1950 when I was having that thought and what it is today, you would say a certain number of things have fallen apart. We have forgotten how to do some things.

GRACE: So your theme is the stuff of the world. All the stuff and how it fits together. And please take us further into this book. This is *The Figured Wheel*. How many pages does that come to?

ROBERT: Well it's all the books I ever wrote, so it's four books of poems plus a new book of poems, so it's about, with some translations, it's about three hundred pages.

GRACE: Do you like the new poems in this?

ROBERT: I didn't find that there was anything I wanted to cut. I found in putting it together I was as happy with one as with another.

GRACE: That is really nice to look back at your life's work and say "I'm not ashamed of that one." What are you going to read which is new tonight?

ROBERT: I have what seems an appropriate poem to read because this evening I'm going to be at an event presided over by my friend Bob Hass, the Poet Laureate, and this poem is dedicated to Bob and to our friend Elliot Gilbert who died a few years ago. His wife Sandra Gilbert, the very distinguished critic and poet, has written a beautiful book of poems and a wonderful book called *Wrongful Death*, about Elliot's death through the mistakes of doctors, doctors who blundered during a routine operation and they covered up their blunder and lied about the cover-up. Elliot loved jokes very much. I like jokes too. This is a kind of an elegy but it's an elegy with a couple of jokes in it. It was written while Bob was working on his haiku book. I guess I had just gotten a first copy of it. One poem I'll read tonight is " Impossible to Tell" to Robert Haas and in memory of Elliot Gilbert.

GRACE: Humor is important in this poem about death.

ROBERT: You certainly don't get many elegies with two jokes in them.

GRACE: Not really. That's really alive, the things that you put together: the haiku, the content of the haiku, the petals, the characters, the event, the situation. Howard Nemerov loved to put jokes in poems too. But this poem is especially masterful in just its ambition, in its length.

ROBERT: I have never really quite gotten haiku. Sometimes Bob would quote them and beam and grin with pleasure and I would feel like I had to be polite and didn't quite understand why it was so wonderful. And I read the introductory material and the notes in his book and I began to get it. He describes haiku as really part of these larger forms including renga which, as I get it, you say a stanza that has falling leaves or comparative confetti at a parade in autumn—that's an autumn stanza—and then a certain number of stanzas later, when it's my turn, I have to say that the colors of the people in their summer bathing suits are like confetti so I pick up something from you, but in a different season, and that's the way a group of very elegant learned friends will spend an evening together, doing a renga, a collaborative poem. There needs to be a master who knows the very intricate rules of change and repetition. In my own culture, I realize that the thing most like that is when people who like to tell jokes, tell jokes. And if somebody tells one about a doctor, then there is a second one about a doctor. Somebody has one about a dentist and that segues that the dentist had an Irish or a Jewish accent and that segues into some ethnic vein, and then another theme is picked up and you collaborate in the evening with a certain sequence of poems or jokes.

GRACE: That particular piece, about Elliot Gilbert, "Impossible to Tell," we have to comment on its style, because when you read it aloud, I thought, well I'm going to hear all the transitions he makes as he does this. I couldn't do it. I couldn't pick out your transitions, and I think that means it's pretty seamless. Now, of another poet's work, you once used the phrase "perfected by style," I think. And I can't remember the circumstance, but I thought then that style was very important to you, in that it is your safety net. You do everything, you do anything, in a poem, but your style pulls it off and I think you are quite impatient, perhaps, of others who may not do that.

ROBERT: I'll plead guilty to impatience as a deep character trait. I think what holds a poem like this together for me, if it's held together, is largely meter. This one is in iambic pentameter, and iambic pentameter whatever else it is, can be a very good glue. It is a very good way to hold things together. It's like four-four time, you know.

GRACE: You can do a lot of things in it. Did Sandra like that poem?

ROBERT: Before I published it, I did in fact—before I showed it to Sandra—send it to her son Roger to see how he thought Sandra would feel, and then I sent it to Sandra and they both liked it quite well. My friend Peter Sacks, the poet, has written a great critical book about the English elegy, and I told him first about sending it to Roger and then to Sandra, and he said "What were you worried about?" I said, well, you know if you've lost a beloved spouse, then read a poem in which there are the words "really dead" and they're a laugh line—I said it gave me some trepidation. And Peter who had written a book, a great book, about elegy, said a wonderful thing. He said, "'Really dead,' that's the point of all elegy."

GRACE: What of your autobiographical poetry, Robert Pinsky? I'm thinking of your poem "Night Game." Do they have a high school named for you in Long Branch yet?

ROBERT: There are two or three Robert Pinsky schools in Long Branch. They're all reform schools. Long Branch is the birthplace of many interesting people. There was a bunch of Jewish storekeepers in downtown Long Branch on Broadway and I think the grocery store was the Grossels', and they had a son who grew up to be Jeff Chandler, and I think it was the hardware store where the son became Meyer Abrams, M. H. Abrams, the literary critic, and it was another store where the pianist Julius Katchen was the son, and the dress shop was called Estelle's and that was Norman Mailer's aunt. And my grandfather had the bar.

GRACE: And how long did you live in New Jersey?

ROBERT: I lived in New Jersey really until I was twenty-one.

GRACE: So you went to school, high school.

ROBERT: I went to high school there.

GRACE: Elementary school, all the way.

ROBERT: I had the same homeroom teacher as my dad.

GRACE: Same house? You lived in the same house?

ROBERT: No, we lived originally in a kind of apartment. We lived in a largely black part of town in an apartment in a two-family house until I was around thirteen. When I was thirteen, we moved to a more, slightly up to the middle class, more respectable part of town.

GRACE: How many Pinskys were there?

ROBERT: I had a brother and a sister as well as a mom and dad.

GRACE: These are little-known facts, you know. They are not in your *Contemporary Authors* I'm sure. And then you went to college. Where?

ROBERT: Rutgers, the State University of New Jersey, where as I mentioned I was fortunate to study with Francis Fergusson, and my freshman English teacher was Paul Fussell.

GRACE: And at the moment you felt things exploding, had you always known that you were a poet?

ROBERT: I was ambitious to be a musician when I was in high school. I was a saxophone player. That was my dream.

GRACE: Do you still do that?

ROBERT: I do it again. I started around four years ago, I started playing again. But I had a twenty-five-year hiatus in between when I didn't play.

GRACE: So from Rutgers…

ROBERT: Then I went to California.

GRACE: And you started writing in the '50s actually, didn't you? No let me see, the first book was in 1976.

ROBERT: I'd written songs in high school, but I think I started calling them poems in my freshman year. I graduated from college in 1962.

GRACE: And your first book came out at what date?

ROBERT: Not until 1974, I guess.

GRACE: And that was *Sadness and Happiness*. At that time, could you imagine that you would be translating?

ROBERT: No, because I didn't know Italian. So it didn't occur to me. Later at Stanford I did pass an exam in Italian on the basis of having studied Latin and Spanish. No, I didn't think of myself, and still don't think of myself, as a translator. And this project, I say—some of my friends say it's a joke they're tired of—but really I'm a metrical engineer. I'm an extremely good metrical engineer.

GRACE: I understand that. I think that's clear, but I think you're a little too modest about that, and we know it's a little bit more than cogs in wheels. You were once called "the best young poet under fifty years of age."

ROBERT: They can't say that anymore.

GRACE: In 1983, you wrote *History of My Heart*. That's a pretty brave title. You know it was like baiting the people to come at you. It's almost like A. R. Ammons writing "Garbage."

ROBERT: I think at the time *An Explanation of America*, and *Sadness and Happiness*, and *History of My Heart* were written, a lot of books were given names that were images, physical images, and using the abstract words in a way was a kind of gesture of defiance or contrariety—if there is such a word as "contrariety." It was an attempt to be contrary, partly.

GRACE: You're a pretty rebellious guy.

ROBERT: What a sentence to say. Yeah, I am pretty rebellious. You could say that in some ways. In other ways, I'm a professor.

GRACE: That's true. And remember they say "He's neoclassic." Also, no one talks better about poetry than you do, and so I was just wondering if you would illuminate all these airwaves and just answer a couple of basic questions. For example, you have been called a "modernist." What do you think a modernist poet is, and would you just name a few of them who are your favorites?

ROBERT: I guess I am loyal to the modernist, the classic modernist—who I'm not saying a postmodernist wouldn't be, I don't know. Terminology is not my great strong point as a critic, by the way. I've never been very good at terminology. "Modernist" for me first of all just means a bunch of people.

GRACE: Who are they?

ROBERT: Pound, Eliot, and William Carlos Williams. And for me, Yeats and Frost. A lot of people would disagree. And it has to do with a generation of writers, I guess born largely in the 1880s and 1890s, maybe as far back as the 1870s, who can only be compared with the generation—I think the generation of people who were writing in 1590 and the early seventeenth century for the just brilliance in innovation and ebullience and discovery of how they change ways of making poems. They just happen to be two great periods.

GRACE: Wallace Stevens is one of your ghosts, would you say? Influencing you?

ROBERT: Yes, certainly, absolutely.

GRACE: I ask you these things because over the years you have been called a little bit of everything. And one person compared you to Richard Wilbur in your writing. Well, there are some passages of yours that are rather elegant and classic and so I can see that too. So I'm sure you don't get hung up on how you are described over the years. Obviously you hardly remember it.

ROBERT: I think you've been reading critics that describe me as being a much more cool and classical and orderly figure than I am. I mean, I'm delighted. To be compared to Richard Wilbur is an honor. I'm not complaining about it exactly.

GRACE: I know. I do actually think that it is true, that critics describe you in a way which is very formal. Their descriptions are very formal and then when one meets you, you are like a person who can take popular culture and put a spin on it and it's really very different from the way you're described.

ROBERT: You make me realize that I've been making a joke and no one has been getting it. If I destroy myself on the way back to the hotel, it will be your fault.

GRACE: Let's talk about another poem just to save the mood, your translations.

ROBERT: How about a semi-translation from a language I really don't know at all. There is a poem in *The Want Bone* called "An Old Man" subtitled "After Cavafy." Since I don't know Greek at all, but I have read the wonderful Edmund Keeley and Philip Sherrard's translation of this poem for years, I do know that it is in a rhyme scheme similar to the one I use. I think I still have the Wilbur notion on my mind...saying how often have I written in a certain kind of rhyme... These rhymes are pretty approximate. So it is with my poem, "An Old Man." There's a case of translating from Greek without knowing the language.

GRACE: Robert Pinsky, your poems always tell a wonderful story. You are a master storyteller. And in that poem, especially. There are far worse things to do in this world than bring a character to life on the page. Thank you. I hope we see you back here at the Library of Congress soon again.

*L*ucille Clifton was born in Depew, New York, on June 27, 1936. She is the author of twelve books of poetry, including the National Book Award winner, *Blessing the Boats: New and Selected Poems 1988–2000*, as well as numerous books for children. During her rich career, Clifton served as Poet Laureate for the state of Maryland, a Distinguished Professor of Humanities at St. Mary's College of Maryland, and a Chancellor of the Academy of American Poets. She died in February 2010, at the age of seventy-three. This interview, recorded in 1999, was her last.

Lucille Clifton

GRACE: We are on location today, at the home of Lucille Clifton, America's beloved poet. I'm holding a new book, *Voices*, in my hand… this is Lucille's new edition from BOA, and we're going to explore this book a little.

LUCILLE: In this book, I'm interested in *naming*, and calling things by their names. What makes us arrogant is believing that we have the accurate name… I got interested in this, in a small way, when I first started writing. I remember listening to the Olympics in Mexico, so that was a lot of years ago. And the United States announcer was calling the place *Mex-i-co*, and the people, the natives of the country, were saying *Me-hi-co*, and the United States guy thought that he was correct… I've always thought that was very odd. After that I started thinking about things like a "cow." That's the example I give my students. How do I know a cow calls itself a cow? And also, what does it call me? I think that's fascinating, and I am kind enough to allow it to say "Lucille," and I guess it's kind enough to let me say "cow" and it shows up. In this book, loss is also something that I'm interested in, having lost many humans of my generation…and yet there's something about that loss. It's your reaction to it that makes you a viable human.

sorrows

who would believe them winged
who would believe they could be

beautiful   who would believe
they could fall so in love with mortals

that they would attach themselves
as scars attach and ride the skin

sometimes we hear them in our dreams
rattling their skulls   clicking

their bony fingers
they have heard me beseeching

as i whispered into my own
cupped hands   enough   not me again

but who can distinguish
one human voice

amid such choruses
of desire

GRACE: I asked for that poem first because that is the voice
and the tenor, and the phraseology that we know so well
from the work we've followed for so many years. But what I
want to say about this book is that it departs from that voice.
This book goes many places Lucille has never gone before,
and I want to analyze that a little bit. First of all, how do you
describe this book?

LUCILLE: Most of my books, I think, are questions, wondering
about things, and sorrow, about which I know a great deal,
having lost my parents, my brother, my sister, two of my chil-
dren, my husband, friends—I think I know something about
loss and what it does, and I often say to people, when people
say, "you'll get over it," well of course I won't. I won't ever get
over it, but I will get past it, and it will teach me something
about how one has to be. Being alive is like traveling a path,
and things happen on it, and you have to bear them, or deal
with them.

GRACE: Or write poetry about them… This book does some-
thing that has not been done before in Lucille's work. She
moves from the personal, political—which we will hear—from
the cultural, into the mystical. And I believe it is among the
strongest and bravest of her works. Let's start with an attack
on racism and capitalism.

LUCILLE: Well, in line with my thinking about names, I was
thinking about those names that we hold dear, and we take
for granted. These are in their voices, and I do voices I think

pretty well. Or well enough, at any rate. This is called "aunt jemima." She is speaking.

aunt jemima

white folks say i remind them
of home   i who have been homeless
all my life except for their
kitchen cabinets

i who have made the best
of everything
pancakes   batter for chicken
my life

the shelf on which i sit
between the flour and cornmeal
is thick with dreams
oh how i long for

my own syrup
rich as blood
my true nephews   my nieces
my kitchen   my family
my home

LUCILLE: This is called "uncle ben," and he is talking.

uncle ben

mother guineas favorite son
knew rice and that was almost
all he knew
not where he was
not why
not who were the pale sons
of a pale moon
who had brought him here
rice   rice   rice
and so he worked the river
worked as if born to it
thinking only now and then

of himself   of the sun
of afrika

LUCILLE: You know, a lot of people came to some states because they knew how to grow rice. And they were in Guinea, which is Africa—a name before Africa... And if that's what you're born for, that's what you do. Here is "cream of wheat."

cream of wheat

sometimes at night
we stroll the market aisles
ben and jemima and me   they
walk in front   remembering this and that
i lag behind
trying to remove my chefs cap
wondering about what ever pictured me
then left me personless
rastus
i read in an old paper
i was called rastus
but no mother ever
gave that to her son   toward dawn
we return to our shelves
our boxes   ben and jemima and me
we pose and smile   i simmer   what
is my name

GRACE: This is the art that Lucille has cultivated her whole life—the persona poem... And in that poem, look what she does with product placement. Look what she does with advertisement. In three poems, in less than fifty words, she takes on egregious and painful subjects in American history. Do you think that people understand your poetry to the extent they should? Be honest, do you? I mean, it's more than just compact poetry.

LUCILLE: I don't know. I'm not sure I do. But I do know that I feel it is dishonorable to not recognize, if you're going to give something human-ness, to not recognize it as human. For instance, when I think of my poem "mataoka," it is like that. Pocahontas was not her name. It was a kind of nickname. And I had students—once they had seen the movie *Pocahontas* and then gone to the Smithsonian to see the painting of her there—come back and tell me that that wasn't Pocahontas because they had seen the movie. Now, these are people who are adults. And imagine saying that wasn't her because they saw the movie. I reminded them that it was animated. There weren't any artists around there drawing the woman when she was alive. Also, the whole idea of the romance with John Smith? She was a young girl; John Smith was hundreds of years old—I mean, I can believe it of him, but I can't believe it of her. I don't think she was in love with him. Anyway, Mataoka is the actual name of Pocahontas.

mataoka

in the dream was white men
walking up from the river

in the dream was our land
stolen away and our horses
and our names

in the dream was my father
fighting to save us   in the dream
the pipe was broken

and i was leaning my body
across the whimpering
white man

if our father loves revenge
more than he loves his children
spoke the dream

we need to know it now

GRACE: There is a way that you tell a story that I want to elucidate... What I finally understood from A. B. Spellman's book about the great jazz musicians [*Four Jazz Lives*]—and it's nice to know technically why we love certain poetry; it's nice to understand—I saw that you do what Ornette Coleman does, and Cecil Taylor. They know the melody, but they play the chord on top of the melody and under the melody. And people might want you to write long dense poetry, with all the details, you know, like they yelled out to these musicians, "Play on the tune so we can dance to it." No. The thing is that you are playing on the tune.

LUCILLE: That would never occur to me, Grace, that this was happening. Though I love jazz. I love jazz.

GRACE: I believe it is so much in you, I think that jazz is so much a part of you, knowing it the way you do, loving it the way you do, that you do to jazz what Sterling Brown did to the blues. I think that you are doing this, and somebody needs to tell about it. Somebody needs to tell on you.

LUCILLE: All right, tell me too. That's interesting.

GRACE: It's the way you space the things; the way you're not afraid to do it differently. You're not afraid to change your point of view in the middle. You're not afraid to take off on a riff. Well, let us go somewhere else. Let us go to another one of your people poems, the one about the coal miner.

LUCILLE: My husband died, actually twenty-five years ago. A long time, you know, twenty-five years ago. Anyway, this is the last thing he said to me. And it was a difficult time. We nursed him; my kids and I nursed him at home, and we had a lot—he had a spiritual center in Baltimore, and he did a lot of things with yoga, and with healing, and that sort of thing, with Eastern religions, Eastern ways of knowing. He was also quite brilliant. He was one of the planners of the African American Studies Department at Harvard, and worked in that department at Harvard—taught there.

GRACE: Let us name his name.

LUCILLE: Oh, Fred Clifton. I'm smiling. It's been twenty-five years. Well, he was so funny. The kids and I talk about him and laugh a lot, because he wrote a children's book for instance, just because I had written one. This poem is titled "you have been my tried and trusted friend."

"you have been my tried and trusted friend"

said the coal miners son
to the chippers daughter
then turned his head and died
and she and their children rose
and walked behind the coffin
to the freeway
                    after a while
she started looking at
other womens husbands other
womens sons but she had been
tried and trusted once and
though once is never enough
she knew two may be too
many

GRACE: What a last line. The thing I wanted to point out here is the woman's sensibility, which imbues all of this work. It's like your ying is really with your yang. You've got a lot of ying, honey. Really, you're a lot of woman; there's a lot of woman in Lucille.

LUCILLE: Get T-shirts! I'll wear them!

GRACE: I love that. Let us go to one more poem that I want to make sure everyone hears, and that is "to maude."

LUCILLE: My dear friend Maude Meehan was a poet in Santa Cruz, where I lived for a time. I taught at UC Santa Cruz for a time. And Maude was a poet there, well known in that area. She was a dear friend and a fine poet, and she used to live in Buffalo, though we didn't know each other then. During the Vietnam War, Maude used to drive—hide guys in her trunk, the trunk of her car, and ride them over the border into Canada… And she looked so much like everyone's grandmother—white haired, big kind of sweetheart lady. She was tough though. That was a tough broad.

GRACE: I knew her.

LUCILLE: Yes, you knew Maude. Ah, she's special. She used to always call me kid, though she was maybe five years older than I.

> **for maude**
>
> what i am forgetting doubles everyday
> what i am remembering
> is you   is us aging
> though you called me girl
> i can feel us   white haired
> nappy and not
> listening to marvin
> both of us wondering
> whats going on   all of us
> wondering   oh darlin girl
> what   what   what

GRACE: Do you see how she knows what not to say? She trusts the reader so much. Lucille goes right from heart-to-heart connection, and I want listeners to get this book, to notice the space in that poem. I want to tell you, there's nothing like a good space… There will never be a book by Lucille without her family. It mentions her mother, father, aunts, uncles, nephews. But we go then into a part of Lucille that I have seen before, but not seen *published* before. This is a set of meditations, which…take eloquence of the highest skilled mind, beyond thought, and it is pretty hard to go beyond thought, and still use words. So these are meditations, and perhaps you could just set this up for us.

LUCILLE: Well, I saw titles of a group of meditation aides: *The Ten Ox-Herding Pictures*. It's an allegorical series composed as a training guide for Chinese Buddhist monks. They are attributed to Kaku-an Shi-en, a twelfth-century Chinese Zen master. I did not know the pictures. I had never seen them. But the poems came, and I had only read the titles of the pictures. So these are ten little poems, and the first is a beginning, sort of an introduction, and the last is an end. My son, my eldest son, who's no longer living, said to me when he read them, "Ma's writing about bulls and livestock now. What next?" And I said, "You know, she writes about what she writes about."

a meditation on ten oxherding pictures

here are the hands
they are still
if i ask them to rise
they will rise
if i ask them to turn
they will turn in an arc
of perfect understanding
they have allowed me only such
privilege as owed to flesh
or bone   no more   they know
they belong to the ox

LUCILLE: I should say I was born with twelve fingers. That's not metaphor. I was born that way. My mother had twelve fingers, and my eldest daughter. And so my hands have always, to me, felt special in an odd way, in that sometimes I can touch things, and get a feel for something other than what I have touched. And sometimes I can't and it doesn't matter to me, I'm not *trying* to do this. Also I should say that the ox stands for... I was raised Southern Baptist, and I remember the day I woke up and looked at my father and said, "I don't think I'm going to church anymore." And it was so hurtful to him, but I just felt that that was—that there's so much else, you know, so much else, and that perhaps to connect with that which was divine... I just read something, in *Poets and Writers* I think it was, and it had some photographs. They were talking about this boy who's considered a reincarnation of the Buddha in India or Pakistan, one of those, and the caption was, "Is He Divine?" and my answer was, "Who isn't?" I mean of course he's divine. He likes to be in the woods with long hair. That's his business. That's his way of doing it. But maybe mine is sitting around watching *The Price Is Right*. I mean that can be very divine. I'm at the age where you like *The Price Is Right*, Grace. Anyway, going on.

1st picture
searching for the ox

they have waited my lifetime for this
something has entered the hands
they stir
the fingers come together
caressing each others tips
in a need beyond desire
until the silence has released
something like a name
they move away   i follow
it is the summons from the ox

GRACE: I saw a concert by Miles Davis before he died, and he had a solo piece that was only one single note on his horn. It was startling. He knew what he was doing. And that is what you are doing. This will be understood in the lexicon of poetry. You will be remembered for this. The book is *Voices*.

Josephine Jacobsen was born in Cobourg, Ontario, Canada, on August 19, 1908. A poet, fiction writer, and critic, Jacobsen received multiple awards for her work, including the Lenore Marshall Poetry Prize from the Academy of American Poets and a Shelley Memorial Award for lifetime service to literature. From 1971 to 1973 she served as Consultant in Poetry to the Library of Congress. This interview, conducted at the library in 1995, celebrates the publication of her ninth book of poetry, *In the Crevice of Time: New and Selected Poems*. She died in 2003, at the age of ninety-four.

Josephine Jacobsen

GRACE: Josephine, how does it feel to look at the retrospective of your life within this book?

JOSEPHINE: Well, it seems an awfully long time, Grace. Eighty-eight is a formidable time from which to look back, I can tell you. And it goes actually from my tenth or eleventh year, so it's a tremendous number of poems and it sometimes astounds me that I really have written as much as I have; and I've discarded a great deal. I'm very critical of my own work and I have never sent a poem out to be published—I was going to say that I wasn't satisfied with, but I don't think any poet is ever satisfied—maybe I should say, that I didn't feel was the best that I could do with that particular poem. So I've written a great many more than the large number—two hundred or so—poems that have been published.

GRACE: Some say you are an enduring voice in American poetry, a woman who gives others permission to go on.

JOSEPHINE: Oh, I would be embarrassed.

GRACE: Formalism is an important topic for us in talking about your work. Elegance is one word used in reference to your poetry. What does that mean? If elegance is the way we contain aesthetics within the poem, if it is about style, would you say that craft and form are important to you?

JOSEPHINE: Well it's very important to me. Not necessarily conventional or rhymed poetry but structure in poetry is to me very, very important. The whole question of rhythm, it's like breathing and the seasons and the sun and moon. It's basic to poetry. And I never have acceded to the idea that this is the time to write rhymed poetry, this is the time to write free verse, this is the time to do something else—ever. I have written unrhythmed poetry even early, when I was working on lyric poetry; and today I do some rhymed work. But not in the majority of cases. I've never felt any compulsion so that a poem I'm working on has to take a specific form—other than what it wants.

GRACE: Since you write prose as well as poetry, then we know that you're not in a lock-step mode of thinking.

JOSEPHINE: Well I'm alarmed. I just read today, just this morning where somebody was commenting on the fact that there seems to me an idea among some people that if you take a prose statement and chop it up and print it in irregular lines that you've necessarily created a poem. And though, as I say, I have never been part of a mode or a trend, I do think that craftsmanship is essential in poetry and also structure is essential.

GRACE: Marilyn Hacker said "When I see a...writer...counting syllables on her fingers, or marking stresses... I'm pretty sure we'll have something in common, whatever our differences might be." Is that what this book of "formal" poetry is about? What of your own poems in this book?

JOSEPHINE: I'm partial to one entitled "The Limbo Dancer" about the death of the dancer.

GRACE: I knew you must have written that in Granada where you escaped winters.

JOSEPHINE: It was a totally Granadian experience—and actually the Caribbean is the only place that I think that you still get limbo dancing. And this was very, very vivid to me. And when I came back I was shocked, the next year, to find he was a relatively young man and I am sure this was a perfectly terrible death. Some people even have muscles cut. It's a dramatic, fantastic performance, but it has its own threat and it was very sad that the guests were back and the hotel was back and the sea was back and the limbo dancer was gone.

GRACE: That's an important theme of yours. Beneath the polished surface, danger everywhere.

JOSEPHINE: I wrote in a very, very early poem—and there are not many lines from very early poems I would want to quote—but it said something about the tissue paper between the foot and the plunge. That's how we go through life, over the tissue paper between the foot and the plunge—and that line I will still stand by.

GRACE: We will too. I think Nelson Mandela in his 1994 inaugural address said something significant which I thought about while driving over here. It was—to paraphrase—that we are not afraid of our inadequacy, it is our power we're afraid of. In reviewing your life, do you see your power? And was that what made you able to support all those fledglings along the way?

JOSEPHINE: Well that's rather an ambitious way of putting it, Grace. I think I knew from very, very early on that I was a poet for better or worse, good poet, bad poet, whatever. But I did know that at an extremely early age it was a drive that was not going to stop, that it was something that could be done no other way, and I did know that even when I was a child.

GRACE: You've been called "poet of affirmation." In your canon is a much-quoted poem "Let Each Man Remember." Why do you think it's surrounded with so much interest, and why do people remember the poem so much?

JOSEPHINE: Well, one reason I like it and it has a particular place in my affection is that it is a poem that somehow in its own way has specifically helped specific people. I have had experiences with that poem both from people I knew and from perfect strangers who have written and have said "This helped me to get through something" or "This is something I kept on my bed table," and that is so beyond anything you have a right to expect. The greatest thing that you could feel about a poem is that it really has helped another human being in a really bad time.

GRACE: That is one thing that poets don't always say first, "I've made a difference in someone's life." Yet they do. You've been honored by the Poetry Society of America with the Robert Frost Medal and the Shelley Memorial Award, you've won the Lenore Marshall Award from the Academy of American Poets—a big deal, very competitive. I think that meant a great deal to you at that time. But let's go back to 1971, when you were Consultant in Poetry to the Library of Congress. You gave an air of comfort and conviviality to the Poetry Office. And you commuted from Baltimore! What is it that you thought that job would be before you entered "the halls," and what is it you felt that you could give to that place?

JOSEPHINE: Well, actually that was a very happy period for me. I thought it was a wonderful job. I thought it was a job which was whatever the holder made of it. Some people have said, "What difference did it make?" It made tremendous differences in many, many areas. James Dickey said something that I think is so true. After his tenure, he said the most important thing is possibly that the job has produced an incredible collection of poets reading their own poems. And if you go back and think of the past—think what it would have meant, well, let's say to hear Keats read "La Belle Dame sans Merci" or Shakespeare reading some of the sonnets. It's mind-boggling and a huge net was cast. There is no question we probably have some people in there whose work is not going to survive, but it was a wonderful conception and a wonderful effort and it's going to be a priceless heritage, I think, for the Library. Another thing was that the Library seemed to be a focal point in so many people's mind for poetry in America. I can't tell you the number of young people from other cultures, from other countries, who came into the Poetry Office. The first thing they wanted to know was what was happening in poetry in America. Then they wanted to talk about what was happening in poetry in their own country. I could go on and on about the facets of that job. It was a wonderful job.

GRACE: You had fun.

JOSEPHINE: I had a great deal of fun. At first I was petrified as you are in any new job, especially with the national exposure. It's very terrifying. I had wonderful assistants, Nancy Galbraith and Jennifer Rutland, wonderful supporters in the office, and as soon as I felt empowered (I think that's the word we all use), I began to enjoy it very very much. I was responsible for the poets who came there to read. I was able to do one thing that I wanted to do, and that was to see if we could gather more black poets reading their work there—who were of course invited because of their work—but I thought that could be done and it was done while I was there. And there were so many things that I felt that I could do.

GRACE: I see you with new poems coming out in periodicals all of the time! What do you think about this burst of energy? Is it something which has been consistent in your life, or does it happen in clusters?

JOSEPHINE: My dear Grace, I wish I could describe it as a burst of energy. I think the energy comes from the poems. It's like a baby that's going to be born, it's just going to be born. It's not my energy. I used to have a lot energy but going on eighty-eight I would not say that that's a real possession. But poetry is very violent in its determination to create itself and I think what's happened is I haven't got energy to resist it. So that's the way it works out.

GRACE: One thing you are known for is your perception about human behavior, about people. Before they called it psychology, artists were always able to tab what we did and why we did it and how we treated each other and that's been one of the things that you have been wise about in your work—in your prose I think, especially. There is a poem in your new book, which begins with your uncle. And I mention that because it makes my point about your observing people and how they behave.

JOSEPHINE: I've always thought the term "second childhood" was infinitely pathetic, and during a very very long illness in my family I was so well able to observe it. The poem which resulted is called "My Uncle a Child."

GRACE: I wanted to tell you that our mutual friend Robert Sargent read it aloud to me and we had a moment where we talked about our own lives through this. It is that ability you have to catch the warped, the unnatural, the painful, and to put it within a bigger frame so that it actually comes out about love in the end anyway. And then it makes me wonder about your life, and frankly I think we all would like to know about your beginnings. Mark Halperin once said a nice remark: "schooled in the school of the love of my family." I think you had to come from a very interesting family. Take us back and tell us about the little girl Josephine Jacobsen. In what kind of a household...?

JOSEPHINE: Well, a very peripatetic household as a matter of fact. My father died when I was five years old and my mother loved to move around. She was not a domestic type. She was a wonderful mother and a brilliant and beautiful woman but she was not for digging in roots particularly, and between my fifth year and my fourteenth year we traveled pretty continuously. Our base was an apartment in New York City, but we were in Connecticut often in the summer and in North Carolina often in the winter. Mother was restless if she stayed too long in one place, and then she decided that I didn't need to go to school. I didn't go to school at all until I was fourteen years old. She decided that she should settle down at this stage of my life and I came here and went to Roland Park County School which I loved and where I was very happy. Usually they say if a child doesn't adjust when she's very young and comes into school late and has never had this experience, that it's a very traumatic experience, and I can only say I don't know why it wasn't, but I loved the school. I was extremely happy there and I was there for four years.

Mother belonged to the generation that thought it was important for a girl to make her debut. It was interesting that it was assumed my brother would go to college. The idea of my going to college was never mentioned and I was too dumb at that point to discuss or think about the choices. It didn't seem to be something particularly appealing, and so it was only years later that I realized that there was a tremendous amount I had missed.

GRACE: You must have witnessed a history of poetry in the twentieth century. And what have you seen, where has it been, and in your view, where do you see it going?

JOSEPHINE: Well, one thing that pleases me now is the fact that I think it is generally acknowledged that you cannot say that poetry is disgraced if it is in a particular form or is not in a particular form. I think Richard Wilbur commented on that. He has continued, gallantly, to write formal poetry through all periods and I have always felt that was very strong. And the good news is now I think this "formal feeling," as it's described in the anthology we discussed, is coming up everywhere. My worry is that this too can swing the other way and become a straitjacket. But I don't think people would ever go back to that. So I think it's a very good thing now. The poet can ask the poem that has been given him or given her what form it wants, and discard it if necessary. I have discarded many poems because I found I had started the wrong way, the way different from the way the poem wanted to be written.

GRACE: I'd like to go right now to a recent poem in the *New Yorker* which I brought here to have you talk about. I'm interested in the progress this poem made from your desk to the magazine. It's from July 18th, 1994. "Noon" gives us a tranquil scene, until the last four lines when a frigatebird dives down to its prey.

JOSEPHINE: Well, I am really a much more cheerful person than lots of my poems would indicate, and this particular poem, which I think has often been misunderstood, shows that. It is a poem titled "Noon" about peace, total peace, and of course in the literal sense I don't believe that total peace can exist anywhere. I think what Keats said about negative capability is so important and to me, in the animal world, the nonhuman world, we're all tied up in certain experiences and if you want really total peace, if you want a moment when nothing is suffering, where nothing is happening that is bad for any creature, it just doesn't exist. So I wrote this poem in the most pacific environment that could be imagined, and some people immediately grasp what I'm trying to say and others have complimented me, "Oh that's such a lovely, relaxing poem. Whenever I get tight or tied up I like to read that poem." On the other hand, my granddaughter, who is a good poet and a very perceptive person, said she could hardly bear to reread it. She said when the beak comes down, it's awful.

GRACE: And that is actually in keeping with some of your themes which are the natural beauty of the world, the terror possible within that beauty, the animal and bird life which you've spent a life observing—all topics for your poems. Your primal attention to the other species—the animal kingdom is key in your writing. What is it that draws your attention to the animal and to the bird?

JOSEPHINE: Well actually, the shoe is almost on the other foot. I have always been dumbfounded that anyone can move through life in a world inhabited by these multiple, fascinating forms of life and really think and act as if the human were the only living creature there. I'm so aware of these innumerable lives going on around us all the time, that are so inscrutable to us, that we have no bridge by which to communicate except in the case perhaps of domestic animals. But these fascinating lives are going on all around us and are just as much part of the daily world as we are and yet often just totally ignored as if they didn't exist.

GRACE: Let's move now to another poem, which was in the *Kenyon Review*. Now I'd like to ask you, when your editors choose poems, what do you think they like about them?

JOSEPHINE: Well when I wrote this poem I was really doubtful as to where to send it first because it was a very offbeat poem indeed and thought that it might misfire, but it was taken the first time I sent it out with very very warm comments and it's a strange poem. It's called "The Blue-Eyed Exterminator."

GRACE: What form is that in?

JOSEPHINE: Well it's not in any.

GRACE: It's an example of a Josephine Jacobsen poem where you cannot identify the fact that it's really an architectural poem. I think every second line rhymes. I haven't counted through. It's not a sonnet, it is your voice and this is the cadence of your voice. But if I wanted to analyze that, we could come up with the scheme. There are definite rhyme patterns.

JOSEPHINE: There's a lot of interrelation in the structure of the poem. I wanted it to have a certain impressiveness because when you write about death, and my point is we all step on ants every day, the death of an ant is not an obvious subject for a poem—though Robert Frost of course did a very wonderful one on that—but I'm writing about the greatest emperor and that requires to me a sort of formal approach.

GRACE: So you honor your subjects by the house you build to put them in.

JOSEPHINE: There were eight or nine sonnets that came out originally in *Let Each Man Remember*. And when I was preparing this book of collected poems, I went back to them and found I thought they stood up much better than I would have expected, having been written at a very early age. And so I selected three of them that seemed to me to have possibly come off best. This was part of my dream fantasies. I haven't built much with the poetry of dream but this was a place and a location in my mind that was not realistic in the sense of having been physically experienced. It was a fantasy world and there was a thread that went through it. There were seven or eight of the sonnets originally, and the first three from the group are reprinted. The title of the whole sequence was "Winter Castle."

GRACE: What were the themes you were working with?

JOSEPHINE: Those sonnets were written at a time when I was thinking about the possibility and preservation of love in the awful reality of the world and they were poems of refuge, apprehension, and triumph.

GRACE: In regard to how we reach one another, the simple topic of communication is your keynote. In these poems you watch your husband sleep, knowing that there are some places that we don't belong. That's on just the first level of that. But there is the mystery, our inability, the possibility, our potentiality—and yet our distance is all there. So there is a lot of tragedy within the surface of that poem.

JOSEPHINE: Well, the personal end of it was so happy. At that point I was very much in love and I was really wondering if love is something that can be preserved and held in the present world and in the present time. And to my joy I found out that for me it could.

GRACE: What of this poem "Voyage"?

JOSEPHINE: One of my many Caribbean poems. I wandered across the skeleton of a boat, beautifully put together but abandoned, and for years it must have lay in the back of my mind as a kind of symbol of untaken voyages which I think a very sad subject—an untaken voyage. So I wrote this very recently but the boat that started this I saw maybe ten or fifteen years ago…

GRACE: There is so much motion in that poem for the subject of a beached ship. Where did you get the idea of the vines coming through, still growing? "The vines are coming…the vines are coming."

JOSEPHINE: Well, the ship was gradually encroached on from foliage in the bush in every direction. It was almost as an assault on its last intention. You knew that in a few years it would more or less be buried and the vines really, truly were coming. And of course I think that happens in life. As you get older, you know, the vines are coming, the vines are coming, and that moment when the tendril touches the keel, one hopes that the poet stops writing and doesn't produce warmed-over versions of something already written.

GRACE: I don't think you need to worry about that because the critics are saying that the past decade of your writing life is your best. But I speak technically because another poet could have said "covered with green vines," the way it remains, but you knew to make it an action. You knew to make it something impending and you knew to use time. So that the motion we get in a small poem is something that uses the past, the present present, present future, present past, and you take all of those things together—of course I'm sure without knowing it, because if you did it consciously it wouldn't work. I guess this is what comes from writing for a lifetime.

JOSEPHINE: Well I think that's absolutely true, and I think the amazing thing is the gestation time of poems are so absolutely inscrutable. You may suddenly have a poem appear and it's almost in a rush. I don't mean that you don't have to go back and come to terms with details, but it's there. It practically writes it—well, not writes itself—but it's on paper in a matter of hours and another poem like this, the seed is sown and comes to maturity years and years later. I've had that happen all the time. And I've heard other poets agree that it is really very inscrutable, the timing of poems because some take years and some take minutes.

GRACE: Do you keep a journal then and accumulate images?

JOSEPHINE: No I don't, and I know that I should. I know that I probably have lost a lot of things by not keeping a journal. But this just was a germ in my mind and whenever I thought of certain failures in life or certain things or aspirations that were unfilled or voyages people wanted to go on, it came back to that little matchstick abandoned boat on that beach.

GRACE: A boat blessed by memory. I need to ask about the gestation of how long it gets a poem from being accepted to being printed in the *New Yorker.*

JOSEPHINE: Well, as a matter of fact, my experience with the *New Yorker* has been that they are unusually prompt. More so than most magazines. I've heard a lot of people say that they take maybe two years or a poem is held for years before it's published. My particular experience has been the reverse. To begin with, they respond immediately. They respond with an acceptance and a check immediately and after that it has never been more than a matter of months and sometimes weeks. I think it's largely a matter of structure and ability to handle the thing because a lot of very good noncommercial magazines, if you can make that distinction, take a tremendously long time. I mean some of the small magazines really take forever.

GRACE: When Alice Quinn accepted these poems, did she say what she liked about them?

JOSEPHINE: No, she's just been very supportive, very enthusiastic. She's called up a couple of times to say that she liked them. We haven't discussed what made her decide to use them or not.

GRACE: You have said that loss is the mother lode for poets. What can we preserve, Josephine? What can we preserve through your work?

JOSEPHINE: I'm afraid years will have to solve that. I don't know, Grace, at all. I mean anyone who's interested in the poems for any reason will find that time and loss and communication are the three constantly recurrent themes.

GRACE: Another poem here which everyone has read I think who knows your work is called "Midnight Moose." Because that has to do with communication. We get so interested in story there that we don't realize what we're floating on, and that is the adjusted inner rhyme and the extended rhyme in that poem. And I have a feeling that because the poem sounds so easy, it must have taken many, many drafts.

JOSEPHINE: Well I'm very bad. I hate revision. It's a labor I loathe but I practice it always. I don't think I have ever sent a poem out to be published that hasn't been kept on the desk for at least two weeks, possibly a month, because the poem that you read a month after you've written it is not the poem that you think you've written. You think "What! Somebody has come in the middle of the night and tampered with my work of genius. This can't possibly be what I wrote." Because things spring to your eye that you should have seen at first and didn't. And so though I dislike revision intensely—it's like operating on somebody while they're alive—I do practice it always before I let a poem go on its own, for better or worse.

GRACE: Are there poems right now on your desk in various state of dress?

JOSEPHINE: There are no poems on Josephine Jacobsen's desk. I literally at this point do not own one poem or one line of a poem. I have one still coming out in the *New Yorker* but that was written some months ago, so I'm old Mother Hubbard. Absolutely nothing on me. My cupboard is bare.

GRACE: I just wanted to get that on record so we could let you hear what you said later, and then you'll say, "Oh my goodness, did I say that right before those next poems came out." Back to "formalism." In the book *A Formal Feeling Comes* [*A Formal Feeling Comes: Poems in Form by Contemporary Women*, Annie Finch, ed.] you talk about writing poems of "varied formalness" during an era when that was quite out of fashion.

JOSEPHINE: Yes, I think many poets who were really just naturally lyric poets got discouraged during that long period when formalism was frowned on as the kiss of death. But I have felt free, I have always felt free from that kind of compulsion. The one thing I have never done is tailor a poem to the things that were waiting for it. Never.

GRACE: When did Josephine Jacobsen write her first poem and when did she publish it?

JOSEPHINE: I'm not absolutely sure when I wrote the first poem but I know when I published it. When I was eleven years old in *St. Nicholas* magazine. And I have said once before and I'm afraid it's true, that was the high spot of ecstasy in the poetic profession. I remember so well the magazine was coming in at a little kiosk in New York around the corner from us and I was allowed to go out on the street alone, which I was never allowed to do, to get the copy of *St. Nicholas* and to look down and see something that had been intimately inside me in print with people coming up and paying for it and taking it and going away with it. It was the most amazing feeling. I thought, "I'm a professional poet at the age of eleven," you know. That was a special occasion.

GRACE: Did it ever get any better than that?

JOSEPHINE: Well of course, but I mean there were many more reasons, the wonder, really the wonder I think then was more intense than any other time. The wonder that something that I had secretly thought should appear on a street in New York in a magazine. It still seemed to me a kind of a miracle. I got a little more used to that.

GRACE: When you published that first poem and you were eleven years old, how were the women poets who were out on the horizon? Were there very many?

JOSEPHINE: Well if there were I would not have known about it. I really didn't make the acquaintance of poets working until

I was considerably older than that. My mother was one of the most widely read people I've ever known in my life, but poetry was not one of her particular interests, and my early reading was such a melange of wonderful things and awful things and different kinds of things—I mean, Keats and Robert Service, and you know, everything mingled up together. I hadn't sorted anything out at that time at all. But I think I read very little poetry. I mean the poetry naturally came out of me, even though I did not read much poetry as a young child. Mother read to me endlessly and I read all the time, and as I got older I began foraging in poetry. But at an early age I was writing poetry before I knew what it was or why I wanted to write it.

GRACE: Did your mother live long enough to see you gain recognition?

JOSEPHINE: Not to the degree that I have it now.

GRACE: After this new publication, someone referred to you as First Lady of American Letters.

JOSEPHINE: Grace, don't you dare.

GRACE: I can't help it, Josephine. I'm just telling you what someone said.

ther Lives

SELECTED POEMS

$\mathcal{M}$oderation

One cigarette a day
is all my father smoked,
no more, no less, and a
single martini taken
before his dinner. You might
say he was the very soul of
moderation.
At eighty, he swallowed
nitroglycerin pills
not to trouble anyone,
first driving to the hospital
to park his car in the lot
happy that his papers were
lined in order at home, no inconvenience to family or
neighbors, no stepping over
the body.
I feel that last moment
as a loud sound written
beneath his life,
a bright spectacular moment
somewhat like a whistle,
his heart sounding like a
whistle, blasting high and clear.
a ship just docking from Italy
or a train
at the crossing
where he held my sister's hand
on her way to music lessons,
looking back at me on the porch
in the silence before the whistle.

Senior Prom

*"Life can only be understood backwards, but it must be
lived forwards..."* —Kierkegaard

Before the return of innocence at the end,
Before I asked how can I go on without you,
Before everything cost more than three dollars,
Before my recipe for dilled carrot,
Before I bought them Easter dresses
            but kept dreaming I forgot,
Before running laps around the dining room table,
Before saying where does everything go,
Before a crystal of feeling broke open
            which will not close,
Before my children came spilling out from a wound
            which will not heal,
Before I found I was the past,
Before the long disease set in,
Before my dead grandfather appeared 40 years later
            pale and white to give me life,

One night I wore a gown of blue and white
            in layers and layers,
            pale blue under pure white,

Before I let go of it all to the sky,
Before I'd say I'm afraid of eternity without you,
Before the waters were rebuked
            and we were calm,
Before the earth was replenished
            with warm rain,
Before being torn between wanting to change
            and not wanting to hurt you,
Before the spiritual hydraulic lifted me from danger,
Before my left eye, left breast, left ankle broke off,
Before my heart was left beating on the sidewalk,

Before I disappointed everyone I ever knew,
Before I tried to make everyone in the world happy,

We danced the slow dance together with
          "Goodnight Sweetheart"
       coming from the speakers
And time and fevers do not burn this away.

Grandmother
for Graziella Zoda

What is the purpose of visits to me twice since you've
    died?

Downstairs near a woodstove I hear you
in motion, always working,
a long silken dress—
tight sleeves at your wrist, soft above the elbow,
wide top at your shoulder for free movement.

When we were young you didn't visit—
you never baked a cake that I remember
or babysat or held me in your lap,
you were in the man's part of town running a man's
    business
calling the world to order,
six children behind you
raised single-handed in your large house. You were
moving, always moving.

When I kept losing things like my parents,
    my children, money,
my time and health
why did you appear in my room with gifts painted
red, yellow, blue,
brilliant-colored toys. What
essential fact did you want me to know,
that the body is the essence of the spirit and so
must be in motion?

Now that I've lost my foothold, my direction, my way,
what is your message, strong spirit,
strong Grandmother,
what is the meaning of your dream-present,
a bright clock shaped like a train—
simply that it moves?

Anniversary Party

Usually as soon as we get it we lose it
Like my favorite earring the left one
Life is broken like that to teach us
Then we must play dress-up
But this time
Anger or guilt notwithstanding
We started all over again
Everybody does what she can
For one full day
Then starts all over again
Pulling the knife from the wound
It healed
From my legs which got me out of things
Or from art   which was
Something to do until we die

This time it was different
An unleashed love between us
Evidence of the celestial
A jazz serial
Equal but different   without standing
          In each other's light
A quality of love behind the note
I kept the plums you gave me
Beautiful things
You finally wanted everything I had
Searching the cave   Thank you

Tell us the worst truth
Not that you would sleep with her
But that you'd understand her
Now it was me   forever

Spit in my soup
Water in the mailbox
Blood in my shoe

No more   no more... a retrieval in the search
For reality   back from the dead
Listen mother   listen   I'm happy
I used to pretend they were in my drawer and I just
Didn't want to wear them
Now they are there   I have them   They are there.

Night Visitor

Your gift, Father, was this feeling of sadness,
the one which fuels me, runs me hard, and which,
thanks to you tonight, allows me to rest.
You came in the dark
to bring me peace, and a dream, once again,
where I interrupt your conversation
with my sister,
where once again I interfere.
I overhear you tell of your promotion
asking her for secrecy.
I surely would confront you
and did just that
to find out there was more, that
you would take her where you'd go,
to Mexico. How bad I made you feel.
You reasoned I was busy with my new baby;
and her husband had just died
she had no other man.
It was all understandable, the logic, plan.
This poem is the way back to the dream
through its crooked hallways and scented rooms
it's cracked enamel teapot bright with reality,
to say what could not be forestalled—
how I was a part of it all,
the wanting, the share of it,
the ruining of the air for both of you,
the sorrow brought and left,
but the most important part is the waking now
to thank you, Father, for the feeling
in the night, which said to me
"Rest a while in sadness."
You took the blame by giving me this story.
You always were an excellent provider.

The Returning

I love to think of those
children's books
with stories about
the tiny boat which is
lost
and flows down a stream and
out to sea
finally ending up
in Hong Kong where
another child finds
the bright toy
and plays quite happily
until it is
lost in another river
and winds up again
in the very same bathtub
where it all began
having somehow floated
down the rain spout
to end exactly there.
I love to think of
that returning
however preposterous
when I read your books
and see the places
you have underlined
the words you loved
thoughts
you wanted to remember
starred with red and blue
from farther than Hong Kong
back to me.

Angelo

If I were to ask what you'd like, it might be to say something
kind about you,
mention something from the past remembered with love.
And so I do. Spaghetti sauce on the bus!
You getting up at dawn to cook it, I carrying a pot
across two states to Princeton, New Jersey,
where my professor lived
and where
students met to read their poems
eating the sweet red specialty
lugged up and down stairs under a huge lid.
No one could buy that kind of cooking, at least in those days,
although now of course
there's a restaurant on every corner.
I don't know how I asked you, Father, to prepare this dish
or whether in fact you offered it knowing
your meal was rare in American houses.
You remained at home that day while I entertained.
I think you hoped to hear them say how sensitive you were,
a loving father, and so they did admire you this night, poets
heard by candlelight, a fireplace, a stove.
In a different room far away, you most likely wished I'd say
they liked it, Italian food, something different for me to
share. Perhaps
I would say good of you. I'll bet you went to bed easily: *This
time I've made her happy.*

A Day at the Fair

Because I missed you so much
I entered the contest.
It was easy.
The only requirement was that I cut a heart
out of the center of my head.
It would grow back.
Even if our teeth touched
when we kissed the other contestants
we'd get a chance for second prize.
I couldn't wait.
Besides, who doesn't like a picnic?
The Chinese man was playing a violin; all
our words were kites flying in the wind.
It's OK I assured the woman next to me
They're all arbitrary anyway
and they don't always mean what they say.
She borrowed my main ingredient
in gratitude.
I didn't care,
because each man there was to choose
the woman he wanted to feed him a cherry
on a silver spoon.
My man stuck his thumb in the spoon
and popped it right in his mouth before the start.
That's why I lost the contest.
But before I could enter the pain
of the lesson learned,
you were there in the chair on the stand by the band,
with the back of your neck just right,
ready for kissing,
and a doll with paper wings won, just for me,
in your hands.

Morning Poem

Each of us has a pond. Mine is deep. I sleep beneath
the water in a silence so clear
the bloom of desire melts from me,
lightning turns fire to the water of pleasure.

Fish are jumping in my heart,
no, they are real fish dreaming of me,
no it is not a dream,
this is a real heart.

Carciofi

One by one things fall away,
everything but the sweet earth itself.
Already this year he has watched the nest's
careful brush of twigs lose a summer song.

He leans his bicycle against the tree. Tuscany
never changes, they say, but the mountains
seem small, each season, as he goes north

toward Pietrasanta. Only carciofi remain the same, clustered
to the earth. Year after year, this time, the tough fruit
is left for the last of those who want it.

My grandfather picks them here, although he
is not a farmer, he knows where on the stem
to reach. A scholar who saw the world as
a work of art, he holds them like this,

carries them back to his small apartment
past the piazza, behind the university wall.
Pisa. Can you see the dirt on his hands, as he
cups them close, their hard skins,
dusty particles beneath his nails.

What moved him to hunger, and when, that night
we can't know, but that he ate carciofi, the diary
reveals; a plant flavored with olive oil.
Maybe after the lamp was lit, a tiny flask

of oil was brought out, pressings
from a vat near grand Granoia. Adding
salt from a bowl, the mineral
makes a fragrance rise, enough to move him to
open a small window and, by luck, hear a nightingale.

Later he will lean over his drawings. But right now he
puts the finished leaves in a bowl. This is the man who
imagined the gas-driven tractor which would
someday ride the fields of uneven ground.

Tonight there is only the vision of a vehicle
in his head, for he feels refreshed after dining.
How strange to rest, brushing his hand across the
linen, smudging it, without thought.
Il paese della meraviglia. He will
visit the farm again, take from his fields.
But for now the mind feasts on what the eye has
seen, villas with ochre walls, pink terra-cotta roofs,
factories with old doors, the ride out of town
pedaling past olive groves, apple trees pinned against

fences, pruned grapevines ready to burst,
covers pulled taut over seeded ground, the sun traveling
to the sea, peaceful snow on the mountains.
Everywhere he looks, the land ready for a new way to harvest.

Advice Regarding a Field of Reindeer in the Snow

If your husband is sleeping, you
can leave him a message and go in
the airplane with the mysterious pilot,
just for an hour, to land in strange
cities, farmlands, perhaps with
wet leaves and wooden
houses, with ruffled curtains.
You may walk to the edge
of what you thought was a forest,
and look through a thick wall of ice
with a gigantic hole and see
field after field of reindeer brushed
with snow, standing still,
how beautiful, like frozen statues,
cold and silent, each staring straight at you,
line after line of them,
a sight you'd never have seen
had you stayed home. You'll never forget it,
but remember to leave a note, before you go, or
your return will be bleak,
it will ruin everything: trip, field, reindeer, snow.

Water on the Sun

for Candace Katz

We both knew it,
that every mother has the same child,
and so every loss is the same loss.
There had been no music before them,
well not exactly the same music we've known,
soon it started up, singing a little song that went like this:
"Inside every hello is a goodbye"
then the music went right on
just as if nothing had ever happened.
We said their names over and over until they had no sound.
Before that, before we knew them, we had felt safe.
Do you remember? Ever feeling safe?
They arrived, and grew, and turned away,
and when they turned back
everything was changed.
We always knew it was coming,
from the first time their bones were claimed and named,
formed and polished, inside us, even then we knew.
They arrived wearing their bodies lightly on them,
with their entire lives lying in wait to tell
what would be known about them.
The minute they were born—that second—
that's when we took their faces for our own,
while underneath, did you realize—as I do—that
underneath the ice the great swimming was already
underway, away, even before this story began.

How a Poem Begins

It's a little thing. Could be
the long O's in Kosovo, or
a woman
alone in the street
after the hurricane
sweeping Honduras.
Perhaps we tell of the child
beneath the flood or
the sound of the wind
in New Orleans, or
the rubble of Afghanistan.
They say poetry is insignificant,
such a tiny voice
no one can hear.
That's why we write of such
little things, insignificant things.

Pinecrest Rest Haven

In the Pinecrest Rest Haven
Mrs. P doesn't know her husband,
Mr. P doesn't know his wife,
but there they sit in the morning sun
waiting to be noticed.
Inwardness is not what God wants
so she adjusts her chair
and moves to where he sits looking at
the center of the rose—examining it for origins.
They introduce themselves, each day,
shy at first, careful so as not to harm.
Leisure and light favor them.
They both like cats.
Both agree it doesn't mean
that's all there is to value. Oh no—
and so the conversation grows. He
plucks, from time to time, some petals—
pulls them off. Infidelity is absence
of desire. This, unspoken, but they seem
to know to stay away
from others walking by. The ground shifts
beneath their feet when names are called. It scares them.
Giving up a fixed view, they think of each other at
night while lying in their separate beds. They
wonder about their strange talks, having the same memories.

Tomorrow in the Sun Room, tomorrow, there'll
be so much to do, with that old friend, that old
friend she met just today, Mrs. P thinks.
Not all parties are for young people. Maybe,
she could run a finger up his arm and
maybe end up in his hair. It
would feel so good. In the fading side of evening
she didn't look her age, the mirror said. She
couldn't quite think of this mirror's name
and she didn't even know the face it had. When breakfast
was over there would be that nice old man, Mr. P,
who seemed to like her. The reflection said
not from loving but being loved. Where'd they get these
    mirrors?
She'd carry everything that she had in her drawers
and show him. Then he'd understand who she was.
He was once invisible, he'd told her that, although quite
well brought up, he added. Once he asked
if it'd be all right to open his shirt
and show her he was a person? He thought
it would make him more noticeable
(not especially from loving but being loved).
He thought she didn't look her age, whatever it was.

BE CAREFUL, Muriel told Coco. When you look
in another direction, that's when you fall. They stood outside
 Mrs. P's door.
Talked loud about her...accusing her of having implants.
By now they should be ruptured,
by anyone's calendar, Coco shouted through the slatted
 door.
Muriel said big-breasted birds were known to fly high.
Archaeology digs found fossils with big breastbones
once flew. She saw it on Channel 12. Mrs. P knew they were
 after Mr. P.
Not allowed to smoke, they still held pencils like cigarettes,
rubbing against him in doorways like bony condors. Coco
 raised her voice
and said *Some people think their shit is pure white*
like icing on the wedding cake. SOME PEOPLE THINK THEIR
 TUMORS
ARE PEARLS, Muriel added. Mrs. P swung open the door,
massive and majestic. Hello, Piss. Hello, Vinegar. I'd like to
 share something
with you. ME! Then she threw Coco's purse over the balcony
 because
there are worse things to lose than your life, Mrs. P knew.
Muriel suddenly became as eager to please as the three
 o'clock sun.

Perhaps they were meant to be together
after all; it looked like he stumbled into her room, or tripped
on the pink rug there in the doorway. It seemed he was
pretending to tie his shoe and fell into her room.
Apparently he was losing his footing when he fell
on the bed beside her, coming down hard, almost on top
without explanation. Maybe this was love, she thought,
his square shoulders pinning down her breasts, his
stubble against her chin. Just because his organ was
lying on her open hand didn't mean she'd hold it,
but she did. Years of failure between them, like a flaccid
mushroom pressing down. He thought he never
wanted to sleep alone again.
She worried she'd never sleep alone again. When she
was lying there just looking at the palm trees outside
the window, she'd close her eyes and feel tiny angels
behind each lid, then behind her ears, down through
her veins, her stomach. She thought of a big angel,
much like a furniture cover, dropping down on
top of everyone she wanted to help. In this way
she went to sleep.

Denial and insistence looking so much
alike, Mrs. P was damned if she knew what to do half
the time. If someone is wrong and has to be right
about something, it's a problem. Like him running
down the hall naked and her calling the nurses' aide.
The way he sees it, he's free and there's
nothing to be embarrassed about, to the wrong.
The way he sees it also, Mrs. P just has to be
in charge of everything going on in that hall. If they
want him to wear clothes, they'll have to write it down.
It's not in the rules. Mrs. P listed twenty parts of the
human body known and shared by users. He'd
written twenty-one once but lost that scrap of paper.
Mrs. P says it's OK if you're in the garden
or tending the flowers naked, but inside is no
place for it. Mr. P says there are twenty-one
words for the body (probably twenty-two if he could
find that paper). Mrs. P has a scene
in her mind where she apologizes to the
tomatoes and the lettuce for sending him out that way.
Mr. P's mother had once said of him: when he was a baby
he woke up saying no. He was naked at birth.

Mr. P decided to hang a bell outside
his door. When the Mrs. was happy, she'd ring it.
This way he'd know, and in his way they could go on.
She always dropped her silverware
on the floor to get his attention,
but if this had worked
she wouldn't always be so agitated. The ladies' aide
said he shouted at Coco "I hate you." But then he turned
and said: "But don't take it personally." See. Cutting up their
meat again. That day Mrs. P went to tell him "thank you" for
pushing Coco and could he please push Muriel
when it was convenient. There was a crowd outside his door.
Mrs. P quickened, rushing her way through, squeezing and
        shoving.
He sat up in bed when he heard her voice.
APRIL FOOL! She loved his humor,
pretending to be dead to get on her good side.

              Standing on the balcony outside
the dining hall he knew he loved her. The sun slanted
in, lighting her deep burgundy hair. She was kind to
him, holding the elevator door more than once.
Besides, she knew all the words to "I'm in Love with You,
    Honey."
Even verse three. He asked her to marry him.
She reminded him they were already married. Oh that's
right because they had the same pictures in each
room. What could he do
to make her his again? Twin baseball caps with PINECREST
on them! He'd seen them in the corner store
(open Wednesdays, 2–5)
they wear them to classic movie night (Thursdays, the
bulletin board promised). It was *The Heiress* again, every
Thursday. No one seemed to notice from week to week.
No matter, Mrs. P always loved the scene where Olivia
ascended the stairs carrying the gas lantern,
head high… the guy knocking at the door,
knocking and knocking. Mrs. P walked high every Thursday
after that. They'd wear their hats,
and later the accordion man would serenade the whole place,
though he only had one leg. No one mentioned it to him.

Mr. P decided to announce
their engagement. Some people clapped. Some
woke up. The accordion man played "Honey"
("It's funny but it's true," went the words).
Wouldn't it be fun to have that built into
the grave... an automatic song box, so
when someone stepped on the grass, it'd start
playing "...Loved you from the start, honey...
Bless your little heart, honey...
Everyday would be so sunny, honey, with you."
He'd do it for her so even if she was underneath
the ground, she'd hear and think of him. And
no one else! He felt young and alive with possibility.

Crossing the same river twice,
always crossing the river inside her. How many
trips down to emotion did it take Mrs. P
to reach the baby who missed her? She
asked Nurse if she ever happened to see a baby
in the hallway, would she please let her, Mrs. P,
—Room A104—hold its bare skin against hers,
so the mother-feeling could drink in
from its warm skin.
Across this country of time, the hunger
sharpened.
So when, that night at dinner, they served bread pudding,
she held it against her chest for the warmth of it.

There was no way Mrs. P
could've *known* it was Muriel in the next bathroom stall
when she helpfully shouted to remember to wipe
from front to back, and not the other way around.
Of course the door crashed open, Muriel storming out,
half arrayed, to report the intrusion to the janitor.
Baffling, isn't it. One offers knowledge and wisdom
about personal hygiene and it falls deafly
to the tiles. Sad. On her way out,
the maintenance man appeared with Muriel,
asking about the problem. No problem
but that people love the wrong things in life.
They don't love cleanliness. Muriel was
still sputtering when she called
Mrs. P a dirty Jew. Mrs. P had studied
world religions and spat back that Muriel
was a dirty Mennonite. The poor clean-up crew
had to come in and sweep up the paper.
Later at Quiet Time, Mrs. P learned
that every single person had a soul,
and love could not live in the same body with impatience.
Then the soul doctor left her to herself to "think on that."
What a terrible thought. People went on forever. Muriel for
        eternity?
In the next stall in the hereafter? Well, Mrs. P would just have
to find another bathroom. She didn't
tell the chaplain that, as she smiled so sweet,
a face as innocent as a wide wide door.

One Friday afternoon
Mr. P is walking down Corridor 3, giving everyone
he sees a one-dollar bill so they won't forget him
when he dies. Different people achieve immortality
in different ways; and Mr. P, a businessman, always thinks ahead.
Coco is downstairs doing what the yoga teacher said: *rest like a
bow, walk like the wind, stand like a pine*, but to be honest it
    hurts
her hernia when she goes from the wind to the pine. Muriel
was certain this time she was pregnant, and there she is
in the dispensary again complaining that they don't
understand. Dizziness. Nausea. What else
could it be! And where is Mrs. P? There she is far down
the hall in her green chenille bathrobe with slippers that match.
She waits at the beginning of the end of the floor,
watching the old man come unsteadily toward her.
She'll slip her hand in his, lead him to their bench.
(Hello, how are you.) They'll sit in the slender sun
under the moon-shaped window in the bright white alcove.
Unless it's already tomorrow, they might go down for tea.
Fridays are peaceful at Pinecrest.
When he says he misses Bing Crosby, she'll
say "I know, I know." That's how new memories begin.

Mr. P was sent to the Opportunity Room
because he wouldn't keep his clothes on.
When he entered Room 15, he was
yelling that he didn't like things named 15,
and he preferred a little ginger in the situation.
Mrs. P was already there waiting.
She'd been asked to come
because she wouldn't take her
clothes off. It was hard to give her a
shower. The doctor said "Now is the only
time which exists." She asked if he'd let her talk
about the *now* that used to be. He said no.
She grew more frightened
and held onto her clothes.
She begged, "Can we talk about the *now*
that's going to exist?" He said no. She trembled
with the thought that there was nothing but *now*.
She didn't want it to damage the past, the future.
Music was put on and a helper would
come in soon to hold their hands.
This meant pill time. Slowly she came
to like the way the light
came off the palm, how Mr. P nodded in his chair,
soft, pink, and naked,
how he looked up and winked his drooping eye.
No, it was definitely a call to her, as if he knew who she was.
Sometimes she'd see an angel outside the pane of glass
    looking in.
She was scared it came to get her friend, Mr. P.
She looked again and, now, there was nothing outside but
    the present.

Release

Forget what I said before—
It's evening in Tuscany.

Someone is making bread that will not grow stale,
others are picking carciofi.

The moon won't speak one word,
so covered with the moss of clouds.

I know someone who died, but stays.
I would live it all again.

Nothing is divested but the
crepe myrtle that screams pink.

Nothing is enough but the
empty wastebasket where letters once were.

Bluebirds

In the small gray hut of self-doubt where the ceilings are too
      low for you to stand,
by the road where your friend would only drive you halfway
      home,
next to the trench of holes filled with grief and wrong
      choices,
where it's better not to know how you should do things a
      different way,
tulips droop from their vases,
and death has never had so many faces.

That's the time to go out at dusk when even the deaf talk
      softly;
don't look at the hummingbird hovering
afraid of the bubbles rising in their nectar—
bluebirds know of danger, their air made of smoke—
large wings of prey
never far distant—
try to find the bluebirds in their church of air,
star seeds of sound that crystallize, then burst.

Alternate Theories

In answering my husband, I said, "I only
wonder about ideas I can use in

poetry." He said this may be a waste
of wonder. Yes. I realize it's not a fair

market exchange, rationing my thoughts
this way. Here we were walking

in the woods—noticing fern. He said
he could make green herbs grow all

winter long in the kitchen—
the white receptacle by the window,

the constancy of a blue
GloLight—the waters of life dripped

in every day with care.
I said, "I like this. It's lighted

up until morning. Like the moon."
Finally something I can use,

helpful to me—while writing in the dark—
for nothing can be seen exactly as we describe it.

Work Is My Secret Lover

"Jazzmen even refer to sex as work.
Some primitive people believe
That death is work..." —Paul Zimmer

Work
takes the palm of my hand to kiss
in the middle of the night
it holds my wrist lightly and feels the pulse
Work is who you'll find with me
when you tiptoe up the stairs
and hear my footsteps through the shadows
you'll see me lift my arm
to stretch and then lean down
to put my head to it
Work threatened to die once
for all that was left unsaid
so I took to it like a young bride
flushed with excitement
adultery too yes I admit it
on all the holidays
when others gathered at the table I was dreaming of it
making love to the movement of paper
the words from my lips
the feel of it
sometimes when company came
I'd throw a tablecloth over my Work and set the plates and
everyone acted as if nothing were visible
pretending I was the good hostess that I was
while on the Christmas tree Work waited patiently
among ornaments gleaming like a groom
I am guilty as charged
for nothing else could buy my feelings
and why would I sell the only thing that ever loved me the way
I loved back
but my beautiful long-lasting
faithful lover, my friend who will never leave.

Arabia

So you've gone
where you can't be reached
maybe to the Left Bank
working among the troops

There you are holding onto adventure
as if it were the code
for eternal life
pressing on in your khaki
vest through muddy fields and terse
fog, clouds of mosquitos

Maybe you're flying over flaming fields

Never mind, I'll go to Boston
where I know someone
and I'll find a job
I may move to
Jacksonville where we had so much fun

I'm sure you'll find *yours*, whatever that is
while I'm leafing through
these damn letters
yellowing in the attic drawer

And even if I read aloud the book
I wrote for you
Arabia wins

—You weren't put on Earth
to make me happy—
you'll go anyway.

Identification

Upstairs on Warren Street, in the jewelry shop, we watched
the jeweler carve the letters of our names
with all the dollars that you'd saved.

It was silver with my name on the front in cursive swirls,
and yours, block letters on the back.
I was seventeen and we wore matching figured sweaters,
the style, 1950,
blue with white stars, woolen, like sweaters at that time.

Years passed, houses and children came and went and
I forgot the time and money that we spent
        until you died
and then, among your "personals"—dog tags, worn to Laos,
(although you thought it was "just another cruise")—there,
attached to your dog tags, my ID bracelet fixed chain to chain,
to bring you safely home again.

I put it around my wrist and wore it every day
these past two years
until it went away last week. Where it dropped, I'll never
know. I searched every store and drawer, dove down the
swimming pool to reach the bottom. Others helped. I called
each place I'd been and then Cindy bought
a brand-new one which I'll engrave with our old names,
but now I know the sign—I think—
You, Ken, bought it, carried it to sea, and took it back again,
generous Indian giver, saying "I release you now to start life.
You, My Wife," in silver scroll, "are free."

Everything Is Smaller
Than the Truth

Knowing the worst, he is gone,
I still try to learn the way of sleep

while the night pressing down on me
holds its basket of dreams

out of reach. I have
taken loss into account, yet

the border of my skin grows thin
with the white of sheet and the

slivers of light under the door
tying my wish to the moon.

It does no good,
the canopy of thought is darker

is stronger than
prayer keeping time to the beat of my heart,

now it is dawn. What language is this
with its different group of birds

telling me the day, its terrible truth,
is going on before me.

Safety

When you were in the 9th grade and I was in the 7th, you
    were
a crossing guard keeping order at Junior High School
    Number 3. No one
was disobedient when you wore that wide yellow strap
    across your chest—
no one bruised another, caused trouble, or so much as threw
    a stone—
no one cracked a joke about you, a man in uniform. How did
that yellow vest feed your soul to let you know someday
    you'd
fly a plane just to feel the power of a strap across your chest.
    What
liberation—to know how to be in charge—strong and
    capable—
flying through gunfire and lightning again and again to come
    back to me.
Although we were young, you were 15 and I was 13, since
    then, I've never
known the world without you. Now I must be 12.

Mechanical Physics

I never knew how to put two pieces together—
say, the garden hose, for example, its nozzle undetectable.
I flooded the new coffee pot because the sections didn't
    quite match.
Can you imagine how hard it was to convince myself I could
    do anything
with more than one panel—I didn't even try.

IKEA sent furniture in boxes, all marked #44.
I could feel the lessons yet to learn, the escape from reason,
    I could feel
my human failure before UPS left the house.

Now in the lightness of the last of this day,
how do I know who will hold me at sunset?
I cannot make the alive and the dead parts come together,
as we once were.
I cannot match the seams—square the ending.

12:45 on a Friday

I looked in my address book
to see who I was.

The wild cat of the past
is all I saw—

I felt the pages again.
A to Z were poised to my finger.

Midsummer   late winter   early spring
Even the stars have lost their
memories.

The red from the Hummingbird
will show life a little ease—

I almost went fishing on a boat to Key West
but I never called him back.

From the Saucer of Sleep

When the kite of night
Peeled the dark from my eyes
I was wrapped in strings of light
He said in my ear *If*
I've ever torn your heart
Forgive me
I was in human form then
And could not help myself
His cheek against mine
A cocoon of safety
It was *him* holding me again
Although I woke to find
He was only a twisted white sheet
And as I turned
The cotton corner cupped my chin
In the palm of his hand
As he once did
I had forgotten that.

First Year Alone

I took a knife and peeled the fruit
So it will bleed, be eaten, heal—

Scrupulously I gave my best
Flavored by Autumn's sky—

This in my hand is essential goodness
Otherwise the morning is unremarkable
Spiritually desperate even—

What do we want from this idea? Sympathy?
The persistence of what is fatal?
Or appetite, a momentary camouflage of happiness—

In the Beginning
There Will Be an End

Life will never be the same again.
It will have been an average house,
a simple day,
then the future—with your head
under my arm. Or the past.
What's in the room at the
                    top of the stairs?

The elation, pleasure,
one thing at a time,
more than what was to come,
    the unbearable prospects
                    however temporized.
Obvious grieving of course.
We have to stay here, pretending
it won't happen.

Summoning the Moment

The importance of saying this now
is that it can't be said later.

By then we won't remember seeing
the crow in the trail of his cousins,

or remember that, just like us,
he has more intelligence than he needs

for survival.
We won't recall that

something unseen exists beyond
flights into pillars of clouds, and skies of fire.

Suppose you are on your death bed,
will you know all the

names for Love?
We won't remember, then, seeing the blaze

of sounds, toward silence,
when stepping out of this movie

into the ever-expanding
transcendence.

We can write
as if there's no eternity.

This simple narrative, engraved, is all we have,
if truthfully said.

Even birds know that to sing their song
is to summon the moment before flying.

Locator

I don't know why love works. Yet it's
undeniable, every line of it hand tooled

like a finely wrought page.
This is very exciting, the extra beat that my

heart skipped, because marriage is discipline
like an athlete's, with the grace of a dance.

It's stillness and silence, the
end of our differences.

Surely our bodies were always
prepared for it. I was on the

verge of sorrow when I thought of this,
this tissue, this sustaining

legend. Here's the door
that will not close. The outcome is uncertain.

Why do you torture me for explanations?
I only know love is the bed of gold we lie on.

Acknowledgments

*G*rateful acknowledgment for poems and play excerpts from the following:

- *With* (Somondoco Press, 2016)

- *Millie's Sunshine Tiki Villas: A Novella in Verse* (Casa Menendez Press, 2011)

- *Anna Nicole: Poems* (Casa Menendez Press, 2008)

- *Water on the Sun: Acqua sul sole*, translated by Maria Enrico (Bordighera Press, 2006)

- *What I Would Do for Love* (Jacaranda Press, 2004)

- *Pinecrest Rest Haven* (The Word Works, 1998)

- *Trenton* (Belle Mead Press, 1990)

- *Swan Research* (The Word Works, 1979)

- *Scene4International Magazine of Arts and Media*

Permission to reprint Lucille Clifton's poems from the Clifton Estate.

Other Voices, Other Lives: A Grace Cavalieri Collection, is the second volume in ASP's Legacy Series, following 2015's *The Richard Peabody Reader*. This series is devoted to career-spanning collections from writers who meet the following three criteria: the majority of their books have been published by independent presses; they are active in more than one literary genre; and they are consistent and influential champions of the work of other writers, whether through publishing, reviewing, teaching, mentoring, or some combination of these. Modeled after the "readers" popular in academia in the mid-twentieth century, our Legacy Series allows readers to trace the arc of a significant writer's literary development in a single, representative volume.